# WHAT IS
# THE MONARCHY
# FOR?

The status quo is broken. The world is grappling with a web of challenges that could threaten our very existence. If we believe in a better world, now is the time to question the purpose behind our actions and those taken in our name.

Enter the What Is It For? series – a bold exploration of the core elements shaping our world, from religion and free speech to animal rights and the war. This series cuts through the noise to reveal the true impact of these topics, what they really do and why they matter.

Ditching the usual heated debates and polarizations, this series offers fresh, forward-thinking insights. Leading experts present groundbreaking ideas and point to ways forward for real change, urging us to envision a brighter future.

Each book dives into the history and function of its subject, uncovering its role in society and, crucially, how it can be better.

Series editor: George Miller

Visit **bristoluniversitypress.co.uk/what-is-it-for** to find out more about the series.

## *Forthcoming*

**LAURA CLANCY** is Lecturer in Media at Lancaster University. Her research focuses on issues of inequality, particularly 'the elites' and monarchy. She is the author of *Running the Family Firm: How the Monarchy Manages its Image and our Money* (Manchester University Press, 2021) and is a frequent media commentator on the royals.

# WHAT IS
# THE MONARCHY
# FOR?

## LAURA CLANCY

Ⓑ

First published in Great Britain in 2025 by

Bristol University Press
University of Bristol
1–9 Old Park Hill
Bristol
BS2 8BB
UK
t: +44 (0)117 374 6645
e: bup-info@bristol.ac.uk

Details of international sales and distribution partners are available at
bristoluniversitypress.co.uk

British Library Cataloguing in Publication Data
A catalogue record for this book is available from the British Library

ISBN 978-1-5292-3462-6 paperback
ISBN 978-1-5292-3463-3 ePub
ISBN 978-1-5292-3464-0 ePdf

Cover design: Tom Appshaw

For Elmer, Agnes, Ginny and Hugo

# CONTENTS

# LIST OF FIGURES, TABLES AND BOXES

## Figures

## Tables

## Boxes

# ACKNOWLEDGEMENTS

I'd like to thank George Miller for the invitation to write this book, and the incredibly helpful feedback on the draft manuscript.

Thank you to Mum, Dad, Sam, Abby and Ruby, and the rest of my family, friends and colleagues, as always, for their support.

# INTRODUCTION

In September 2022, the coffin of Elizabeth II was placed on display in Westminster Hall for her lying-in-state. In the days that followed, public and media attention turned to the spectacle of 'the queue': an at-times five-mile-long queue across central London of people waiting upwards of 12 hours to view the coffin. The queue had its own Twitter feed, its own weather forecast, and the BBC started a 24-hour live feed of people filing past the coffin to pay their respects.[1] The queue assumed a central place in the media representations of mourning: public grief was made spectacular as a national narrative of sacrifice and pilgrimage, mediated from the centre of the state in London. It was also often presented as evidence of commonality and unity: a nation coming together in grief. This was never more so the case than when celebrity David Beckham queued for 13 hours overnight alongside the public. Sky News' political editor Beth Rigby tweeted that 'in this moment of national mourning, [he] was just like everyone else'.[2] Nationalist spectacle was being used to flatten class politics. Indeed, notions of 'we're all in this together' are directly contradicted by the very purpose of the queue in the first place: to pay tribute to a woman who, by virtue of birth, was given power, wealth and privilege beyond most people's imagination, and throughout her long reign upheld systems of (neo)colonialism, patriarchy, class inequality and racial inequality. In an era where global inequalities are ever widening, myths of commonality erase the challenges of lived experience for the billions of people not part of the 'global elite'.

\*\*\*

The answer to the question in the title of this book, *What Is the Monarchy For?*, might seem obvious at first glance. I'm sure everybody reading this could tell me something about what the monarchy *is*. We can probably all distinguish Buckingham Palace by sight; we all recognize symbols of royalty (crowns, thrones, carriages, for example); and many of us will have opinions on which royals we do and do not like.

But what is the monarchy *for*? This is not such a straightforward question, and there has never been a more pertinent time to ask it. I am writing this book in 2024, at the beginning of King Charles III's reign. His will certainly be shorter than his mother's: he was 73 years old when he took the throne. It also seems likely to witness more social upheaval. The Queen was crowned amidst widespread social renewal after the Second World War; she witnessed the high point of the welfare state and the financial boom of the 1980s. The King reigns in a time of widening global social inequalities, the aftermath of Brexit and the COVID-19 pandemic, the climate emergency, intensifying global political instability, Russia's war on Ukraine, and Israeli genocide in Palestine. As we will see in this book, the monarchy has adapted itself in some ways to the modern age. It has – at least in part – embraced developing media cultures and social media, for example. But it remains at odds with much of contemporary society. Increasing scholarly and activist attention is turning to 'the elites': the world's richest people who are amassing more and more of the globe's wealth, assets and power. Yet the British monarchy remains. Global activist movements protest against violations of democracy, the abuse of power, the hoarding of wealth, racist violence, gender inequality and homophobia. Yet the British monarchy remains. Many former colonies are calling for their former colonizers to take responsibility for the violence, murder, theft, enslavement and indentured labour that has plundered indigenous communities and destroyed democracies for hundreds of years. Yet the British monarchy remains. Indeed, what has often astounded and fascinated me, and partly what drives my interest in this topic, is that even among some of the most radical, progressive thinkers, monarchy is often positioned as separate from these wider issues. A niche subject in the context of multiple global crises, and one we shouldn't waste our time worrying about. I strongly contend that this apathy is part of the reason why monarchy has managed to survive for so long. My project in this book is to demonstrate why the abolition of monarchy should be central to any calls for radical democratic change.

If we look at the fate of many European monarchies, it seems incongruous that Britain still has one at all, never mind still in its ceremonial form. The monarchy has weathered multiple 'anni horribilis' (a Latin phrase meaning 'horrible year', made famous by Elizabeth II in a 1992 speech about a challenging year for the monarchy), abdications, unpopular royals, 'sex scandals', the collapse of its empire and missing heirs. It even came roaring back to life after its actual abolishment in 1650s England. The English Civil Wars between Royalists and Parliamentarians were fought over the balance of power between parliament and Charles I. After Charles I refused to make concessions, he was executed in 1649 and the Commonwealth of England was established, led by Lord Protector Oliver Cromwell. Upon Cromwell's death and his son's brief rule, the Protectorate Parliament collapsed into anarchy and the monarchy was restored in 1660. Many have suggested that the royal scandals of more recent years – from Prince Andrew's alleged sexual abuse of minors to Meghan Markle's experiences of racism – spelled the imminent demise of the monarchy. But it has survived much worse. It has adapted itself to the changing world with more surety than most other institutions in history. We may never see King Charles III behead his rivals on Tower Hill like his forebears, but he certainly enjoys a similar privileged, wealthy lifestyle.

This book argues that the survival of monarchy depends on different forms of power. These different forms operate on various registers, in different contexts, for different audiences and to different effect, although all have the same end goal of ensuring the continuation of the institution. The book is split into four parts. Part I, 'Real Power', focuses on political power in terms of state, constitution and society; Part II, 'Soft Power', looks at the symbolic and economic functions of monarchy; Part III, 'Hidden Power', thinks about the social norms and systems that are reproduced through monarchy, and Part IV, 'What's Next?', considers potential future alternatives to monarchy.

Power is a difficult term to define, particularly when it comes to the monarchy. When we talk about the power of the contemporary British monarchy we are, of course, not talking about quite the same power as that exercised by Henry VIII, who appointed himself Supreme Head of the Church of England, expounded the divine right of kings, and freely executed any dissenters under charges of treason. French Philosopher Michel Foucault referred to this as 'sovereign power', meaning a dominant power or authority (such as the law, a monarch or another authority figure).[3] He argued that in the 18th and 19th centuries, sovereign power gradually broke down and was replaced with 'disciplinary power'. Disciplinary power regulates the behaviour of individuals in a society, and discipline is embodied. That is, we discipline ourselves. CCTV surveillance is a good example: we never know whether the camera is turned on, if it is recording, or if anyone is watching the footage. Yet, generally, we will behave as though we are being monitored. In this sense, disciplinary power is not directly 'top down' from an authority figure like a king threatening a death sentence, but rather power is everywhere throughout society, constantly circulating and (re)producing, although it is inevitably hierarchical. Power is multiple, complex and embodied.

I have called Part I 'Real Power' because political power in terms of state, constitution and society is how we often imagine power in its simplest terms. The prime minister is very obviously power*ful*, for example; able to create law and policy and oversee the operation of government agencies. Likewise, the monarchy, or the Crown, has significant political power and influence, operating at the very centre of the British state. We might also call this section 'hard power': it is tangible and, at least in some part, measurable. In contrast Part II, 'Soft Power', involves values, ideals and culture. It considers how monarchy shapes society through symbolic representation, and in turn how monarchy is shaped by social changes. The role of the monarchy in shaping our understandings of national identity, for example, is intangible: difficult to measure beyond partial polling of the public. But there is significant power in being able to shape values and preferences, and structuring how people understand themselves within the nation state. Part III, 'Hidden Power', deals with powers that are even more elusive. The monarchy has concealed investments and values, through which its powers are reproduced. It owns huge swathes of land, for example, that provide income and rentier power. Or it has connections to colonialism, imperialism and empire that continue to enrich it. These hidden powers are vital to understand the present: how we got to where we are and how the monarchy retains its power. Part IV, 'What's Next?' considers potential alternatives to monarchical futures. What would happen if monarchical powers were abolished? How might this happen and what would it look like? How would power, and the norms and principles on which that power is built, change? Why should we care about abolishing the monarchy?

Each chapter begins with a 'myth' about monarchy: a quote from commentators, journalists, academics, members of the public, or the royals themselves. These examples represent broader shared stories or understandings often repeated uncritically by supporters or defenders of the British monarchy. Over the course of the chapter, we will spend time together breaking down this myth, employing alternative statistics, readings and understandings. There is thus a two-pronged interpretation of the title, 'What is the monarchy for?': first, 'What is the monarchy *thought* to be for?'; and, second, 'What is the monarchy *actually being used* for?'. It is the latter that I hope we can unpack together.

Social justice movements aim to disrupt normative functions of power. The feminist movement aims to dismantle the patriarchy, anti-racist activism aims to demolish racism, and so on. The anti-monarchy movement aims to abolish monarchical forms of power. Our job in this book is to understand how we can do this, and more importantly, what we might be doing it for.

# PART I
# **REAL POWER**

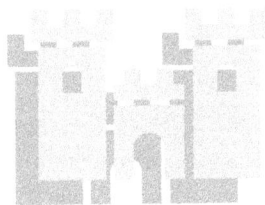

# 1
# STABILITY AND CONTINUITY?

Myth: 'Both a hereditary monarchy and an appointed House of Lords can be justified without doing violence to the democratic principle.'

Vernon Bogdanor and Iain McLean, political scientists, 2010[1]

In May 2022, Queen Elizabeth II's Imperial State Crown arrived at the annual State Opening of Parliament in its own car. It was transported solo because only the monarch, the Archbishop of Canterbury and the Crown Jeweller are allowed to touch it, and then-Prince Charles was taking the ceremony in lieu of his mother, who was unwell. On its arrival at the Houses of Parliament, the crown was placed on the throne usually occupied by the monarch.

The Imperial State Crown symbolizes the sovereignty of the British monarch. In being separated from the physical body of the Queen, the crown's car journey drew widespread attention to the symbolic power of monarchy. When atop the Queen's head, the crown becomes partly just a piece of jewellery, or a part of her expected appearance; for example, we are used to seeing an etching of her crowned head on our money and stamps. When the crown as a disembodied object is put centre-stage in state ceremony its, and the monarch's, symbolic function in the state is brought to light.

One of the best-known accounts of monarchical power and the state is historian Ernst Kantorowicz's medieval political theology of the 'king's two bodies'.[2] Writing in the 1950s, Kantorowicz made a distinction between the 'body natural' of the monarch (the mortal, human body) and the 'body politic' (the symbolic body, constituted by their subjects). While the body natural can die like everybody else, the body politic is transferred to the body natural of the next heir. That means that monarchical power never dies, a concept encapsulated in the cry, 'The king is dead, long live the king'. This offers us an interesting way of thinking about the Imperial State Crown's solo car journey. Media and public commentary are often very engrossed in the status of the monarch's 'body natural'. On this occasion of the State Opening of Parliament, for example, there were countless debates about what was wrong with the Queen's health that meant she could not attend.[3] We see much less debate about the 'body politic': the sovereignty, state power and politics of monarchy that underpins its place in our political and social system.

This chapter considers monarchy's 'official' political

powers and responsibilities as a way of dispelling the myth at the head of the chapter that the monarchy doesn't violate the democratic principle. It shows the role that monarchy plays in the constitution, governance, and in relation to religion and the church.

## A constitutional monarchy

The UK, Australia, Canada and New Zealand operate as constitutional monarchies, with the British monarch as their head. While a monarchy is a state ruled by an absolute ruler (the norm for much of history, and a few still exist, such as Saudi Arabia), a constitutional monarchy is a state headed by a sovereign who is constrained by ministers, parliament and the courts in such a way that they could not become a tyrant, or abuse democratic processes. Political scientist and constitutional expert Vernon Bogdanor summarizes a constitutional monarchy as 'a state which is headed by a sovereign who reigns but does not rule'.[4]

The principles of constitutional monarchy were established by the Bill of Rights 1689, which sought to ensure against monarchs abusing their power. The bill prevented monarchs from suspending laws they disagreed with, raising taxes without parliamentary consent, interfering with elections or the legal system, or having a standing army in peacetime. It also made the monarchy dependent on parliament for funding.[5] The Civil List Act 1697 meant that parliament awarded the monarch annual grants, rather than them being able to spend at will (since 2011, this has been replaced by the Sovereign Grant, see Box 1.1). This all essentially meant that from 1689, the sovereign no longer held supreme power. Rather, the sovereign holds the title with the consent of parliament. And because parliament is seen as representative of the people, this means that the monarch's legitimacy to rule is understood to derive from the will of the people.

### Box 1.1: What does it cost?

It is worth briefly looking at the funding model of the British monarchy versus other monarchies or republics around the world, to understand how constitutional monarchism has developed.

The British monarchy is funded by the Sovereign Grant. This is said to be calculated from the annual revenue of the Crown Estate – a portfolio of land and property belonging to the Crown (see Chapter 7) – which is given to the Treasury in exchange for the monarchy's funding. On paper this is meant to signal a fair exchange, whereby the funding is relative to the estate's annual performance. In reality, however, royal funding is much more complex. When the Sovereign Grant was created in 2011, the calculation was set at 15 per cent. In 2016, the royal trustees (the prime minister, the chancellor and the Keeper of the Privy Purse – the monarchy's finance manager) agreed to increase this to 25 per cent for the next ten years to cover renovations at Buckingham Palace. In 2023, Crown Estate profits more than doubled from

£443 million to upwards of £1 billion, because the estate sold leases for offshore wind farms. This means that in 2025, the monarchy's funding will be about £124 million.[6] Moreover, the *monarch* does not own the Crown Estate, the institution of the *Crown* does, meaning that this connection between profit and funding is merely fabrication. In addition, while the Sovereign Grant accounts for the monarchy's 'official' funding, this is supplemented by other sources, such as security and police support provided by the Home Office, ceremonials funded by the Department for Digital, Culture, Media and Sport, and state visits paid for by the Foreign and Commonwealth Office. All of this means there is a lack of transparency over how much the monarchy costs, because the different sources make it very difficult to calculate.

In comparison, there was some criticism in the Netherlands as the Dutch royal family received an 11 per cent boost in 2023 to reflect inflation, but this puts their total cost at €55 million (approximately £46 million), around £78 million less than the British monarchy.[7] The Spanish royal family receive approximately £7.4 million, the Swedish £11.5 million, Belgian £12.5 million, Danish £14 million, Luxembourgian £16.9 million, and the Norwegian £24 million, making the British monarchy by far the most expensive in Europe.[8] In republican nations, the cost of running the Irish president's office was €4.8 million in 2021 (approximately £4 million).[9]

We should not only be concerned with the cost of the British monarchy in comparison to others, but also the lack of transparency in where the funding comes from.

The terms 'the sovereign', 'the monarch' and 'the Crown' are often used interchangeably, and although they are closely related, they have distinct meanings. The Crown is sometimes used as a shorthand for the state, and in most other countries what we in the UK and the King's other realms know as the Crown would indeed be the state. But it is also much more than this. Broadly speaking, the Crown is simultaneously the government, the state, the monarch and their representatives, and executive power.[10] The Crown also acts as the legal embodiment of executive, legislative and judicial governance, and is a 'corporation sole', a distinct legal entity. Meanwhile, the sovereign is the living embodiment of the state, or the personification of the Crown. Neither of these can exist without the other, so the office of the Crown cannot exist without the office holder (the sovereign). The powers of the Crown are exercised by the monarch, a term which is interchangeable with the term sovereign in monarchies where the authority of the state is formally derived from the monarch (like the British monarchy). The 'king's two bodies' theory becomes relevant again here: the body of the sovereign is simultaneously the Crown (the body politic) and the living embodiment (the body natural), and the Crown's status as a corporation sole means that Crown powers can pass without legal interruption to the next monarch. Both constitutional monarchy and the Crown are 'elusive, shapeshifting and hydra-headed entit[ies] that assume ... a number of different forms', hence the confusion about their status.[11]

In the UK, as head of state the sovereign retains legal responsibility for functions that are central to the political system.[12] These are the monarch's prerogative powers, known as the monarch's personal prerogatives or reserve powers.[13] The formal start of the parliamentary year begins with the State Opening of Parliament and the monarch's speech which sets out the government's agenda for the year (see Figure 1.1). This is also the only occasion when the three constituent parts of parliament – the House of Commons, the House of Lords and the sovereign – come together. The end of the parliamentary year is signified by the prorogation, which is enacted by the monarch (more

**Figure 1.1: The State Opening of Parliament at Westminster**

King Charles III, sitting next to Queen Camilla, formally opens the new session of the Houses of Parliament during the State Opening of Parliament in the Lords Chamber at Westminster, 7 November 2023.

on this in Chapter 2). The Crown dissolves parliament before a general election. The monarch also nominally appoints and removes ministers (including the prime minister) and gives 'royal assent' to primary legislation (more on this too in Chapter 2). Many other prerogative powers are exercised by government ministers as part of the royal prerogatives; for instance, they have the power to deploy the armed forces, conduct foreign policy or make treaties, and grant honours. Some powers are enacted by the monarch on advice of ministers (although 'advice' does not mean they have a choice to ignore it – ministerial advice is essentially binding). But the monarch is the ultimate guardian of the constitution. If a prime minister refuses to resign after losing the confidence of the House of Commons, for example, the monarch has the ultimate power to dismiss them.

Victorian journalist Walter Bagehot famously summarized the monarch's rights as 'the right to be consulted, the right to encourage, the right to warn'.[14] The monarch is consulted on some laws and policies, particularly those that would affect their own interests (for example, their land ownership. Again, see Chapter 2 for more on this). They also receive a 'red box' of government documents each day which they must sign to provide royal assent for, and have a weekly audience with the prime minister. While the content of these meetings is always kept secret (and the democratic implications of this should be questioned), this is likely the space in which they wield the right to encourage and to warn. The weekly meetings are perhaps the best known of the monarch's political roles, and they have been dramatized in fiction often. In the Netflix series *The Crown* (2016–23), the Queen is seen in an audience with Winston Churchill, Anthony Eden, Harold Macmillan, Harold Wilson, Edward Heath, Margaret Thatcher, John Major and Tony Blair. The inspiration for *The Crown* was Peter Morgan's 2013 play, *The Audience*, which centres wholly on a series of audiences between the Queen and her prime ministers.[15] As these are human relationships, this is perhaps the most palatable and interesting part of the monarch's 'body politic', hence its popularity as a genre of royal fiction. *The Crown*'s fictionalization of the Queen's relationship with Thatcher, for example, focused as much on their mutual roles as mothers as it did global politics.[16]

Bagehot's three rights are often misquoted, with the right to be consulted or the right to encourage often replaced with the 'right to advise'.[17] 'Advise' amounts to something quite different from 'be consulted': it suggests an active role in politics, with the sovereign permitted to give shape to policy. According to constitutional norms, it is the sovereign who listens to the advice of ministers, not the other way round. In 1986, the Queen's private secretary, Sir William Heseltine, wrote a letter to *The Times* in which he said that the Queen 'has the right – indeed the duty – to counsel, encourage and warn her government'.[18] 'Counsel', again, inverts the power relations so it is the sovereign advising ministers, and 'duty' rather than 'right' proffers a more active function. Lawyer

Anne Twomey points out the problems that could arise from this 'duty', if monarchs use this power to urge ministers to alter policies that affect their personal interests, as with Prince Charles's infamous 'black spider memos' (see Chapter 2).[19] Similarly, once documents relating to Queen Victoria's reign were released after her death, Bagehot's rights of 'consult, encourage and warn' (which he wrote while she was on the throne) were revealed to wildly underestimate the extent of her influence and reach within government, such as blocking army reform and preventing the appointments of ministers.[20] Likewise, Heseltine's 'counsel, encourage and warn' may prove to miscalculate Elizabeth II's role once documents are released about her reign. In the next chapter we will discuss moments where these rights, and indeed the constitutional role of the monarchy, have come into question because the system has not worked like it is supposed to, or has actively been abused. But the point is that this demonstrates how the monarch's and the Crown's rights are 'elusive'.[21] The key purpose of constitutionalism is to stop the concentration of power in one person or one body, because this can lead to misuse. Constitutionalism proposes a system where one individual or office can provide checks and balances for another. The two offices of a democratic government system – the head of state and the head of government – are meant to provide precisely this function. But, as we will see, this is not so straightforward in a constitutional monarchy.

## The Supreme Governor of the Church of England

Scholar Norman Bonney argues that despite decreasing religious activity in the UK, 'religious doctrines, rituals and institutions are central to the legitimacy, stability and continuity of key elements of the constitutional and political system'.[22] This is because the Churches of England and Scotland could be considered 'civil religion – religion in service of the state', whereby the two Christian denominations are officially recognized as the national expression of religion.

Monarchy is central to this, and the institutions of the monarchy and the church are distinct but tightly interlinked. In his quest for an annulment of his marriage to Catherine of Aragon, in 1534 Henry VIII was declared Supreme Head of the Church of England, and the Act of Supremacy abolished papal authority, breaking with Rome and the Catholic Church.[23] Today, monarchs are titled the Supreme *Governor* of the Church of England, to recognize Christ as the Head of the Church. At their coronation, the monarch must undertake a Holy Communion where they are anointed and crowned by the Archbishop of Canterbury, and the oaths require the monarch to swear to be a faithful Protestant, to uphold the Church of England and, in Scotland, the Presbyterian Church of Scotland. Rather than promising to uphold the constitution, democracy or the will of 'the people', then, it is the church that the monarch is sworn to. A recent review of the UK constitution has recommended that the religious language of the coronation is reassessed before Prince

William is crowned, to better reflect the contemporary moment and the Commonwealth.[24] Foregrounding the monarchy's constitutional role in the oaths would also bring it more in line with other heads of state around the world, like Ireland's president, who is sworn in with the promise that they will 'maintain the Constitution of Ireland and uphold its laws'. This would be more fitting for the politically impartial role of head of state. But in featuring the church so centrally in the coronation, the monarchy's constitutional role is indivisible from its religious one.

In 1867, Bagehot wrote that monarchy 'strengthens our government with the strength of religion' because it draws the 'credulous obedience of enormous masses'.[25] Beyond the religious functions of monarchy, there are parallels in how religion and monarchy are understood. In early modern England, the 'royal touch' referred to a ceremony where the monarch would touch the face and necks of people who had scrofula, because it was believed the monarch had the healing power of Christ.[26] The disease was known as 'the king's evil'. The practice took prominence during the reign of Charles II, which has been attributed to the monarch's need to assert himself as the legitimate king following the restoration, 'uniting throne and altar, while those who flocked to him as healer paid allegiance to the crown'.[27] Queen Victoria's reign was immortalized in the stained glass windows of churches making 'her person and [the] throne a symbol for their ecclesiastical visions'.[28] More recently, Elizabeth II's faith was widely commemorated throughout her life and at her death, with her 'duty' as sovereign often conflated with Christian notions of serving the greater good.[29] In these examples, the monarch is seen to represent the virtues of Christian ideology, and vice versa. Each promotes the other's cause.

Research by the National Secular Society, who argue for a separation of religion and state, found that the UK's investiture of the monarch is the most overtly religious of any European country.[30] In Luxembourg the monarch swears loyalty to the state constitution, and in the Netherlands they swear to uphold law and protect the country. Even where religious elements are present, like in Norway, where the benediction takes place at the high altar in the Nidaros Cathedral, the monarch swears to 'govern the Kingdom of Norway in accordance with its Constitution and Laws'. Elsewhere in the world, Thailand's monarch must be Buddhist, and in recent years there has been a shift back towards the monarch being seen as a spiritual religious leader, with the King representing the 'socio-religious values' of contemporary Thailand.[31] In Japan, the emperor is head of the Imperial House, which makes them the head of the Shinto religion and a central religious symbol.[32] While the examples of Thailand and Japan are very different given the socio-political and socio-religious contexts of these places, the British monarchy's proximity to religion certainly seems more comparable here than it does with their European counterparts.

## The body natural versus the body politic

Anthropologist Cris Shore argues that the Crown fulfils a number of 'social, legal and symbolic functions': personifying the state to give it a human face, embodying morality and legitimacy, acting as a channel for emotion, and being a 'conceptual placeholder' for the state.[33] Many of these speak to questions of symbolism, whereby the monarch acts as a human conduit for the complexities and machinery of state power. This is the story we will tell in the rest of this book. The question 'What is the monarchy for?' could be answered very differently depending on if you are looking at the 'body natural' or the 'body politic'. But while these are distinct, they are also tightly interwoven. It is not that the 'body politic' belongs to the 'serious' realm of politics, while the 'body natural' belongs to the 'trivial' world of celebrity and ceremony. Rather, all of these together are the source of the monarchy's power. One could not exist without the other, and the monarchy would not survive without either.

# 2

# ENSURING DEMOCRATIC LEGITIMACY?

Myth: 'Does not the ideal monarch stand for a higher good and a deeper principle than that of the politician? Indeed, by personifying the nation, the monarch holds politicians and democratic politics to a higher standard. The King or Queen in seeking to stand for all members of the national commonwealth saves us from extremism and the righteous fundamentalism of those who believe only in their beliefs.'
Phillip Blond, political philosopher, 2010[1]

In the last chapter, I outlined how monarchy's constitutional role is supposed to work in relation to government, parliament and the church. In this chapter, I will build on this by exploring not what the monarch and the monarchy are 'supposed' to do, but rather how they actually work, or do *not* work in some cases. The functions of the Crown and the state more broadly are shrouded in secrecy, and the monarchy both promotes and benefits from this. We do not know precisely how or when many of the monarch's constitutional rights are actually exercised. And, where we do know, we see how – in contradiction to what Blond claims in this chapter's opening quote – they are extremely ineffective in ensuring political accountability or democracy, because constitutional monarchy is so limited in its abilities. We'll explore these issues through a set of (relatively) recent crises around monarchy's political roles.

## The prorogation crisis

In August 2019, Conservative Prime Minister Boris Johnson formally advised Queen Elizabeth II to prorogue (temporarily suspend) parliament from early September to mid-October that year.[2] Proroguing parliament is a royal prerogative power exercisable only by the monarch. It is usually procedural and lasts around a week, ending one session of parliament and concluding any unfinished business, before a new session commences. All bills, motions and parliamentary questions cease for the prorogation period, and MPs reconvene when a new parliamentary session – marked by the State Opening of Parliament – begins. Johnson's request for a six-week prorogation was, therefore, extremely unusual.

Johnson's advice to the Queen came at the height of the complex and long-winded negotiations for the UK to leave the European Union ('Brexit'). The negotiations had already seen Prime Minister

Theresa May resign because parliament could not agree on her exit strategy, and there had been heated debates among MPs about the future.[3] Proroguing parliament as Johnson advised would mean that parliament only reconvened 17 days before the UK's scheduled departure on 31 October 2019. Many opposition politicians and political commentators criticized Johnson's move as an unconstitutional and undemocratic attempt to close down parliament, and therefore short-circuit parliament's core democratic function by preventing its scrutiny of the final details of the Brexit deal.[4] However, MPs had no formal means to prevent the prorogation, because these powers are vested in the monarch.

On 28 August, the Queen accepted Johnson's advice and ordered parliament to be prorogued. As we saw in the last chapter, while the word 'advice' suggests informal counsel, the prime minister's advice to the monarch is pretty binding because the monarch's legitimacy derives from the people. Had the Queen rejected his advice, she would essentially be undermining the government and inserting the monarchy into the political struggle between the prime minister and parliament, which could have triggered constitutional chaos given that the monarch is meant to be politically neutral. The Queen therefore accepted, and the ruling on its legality was left to the courts.[5] In late September, the Supreme Court ruled that Johnson's advice to the Queen had been unlawful because it exploited residual royal prerogative powers to prevent parliament from carrying out its constitutional function and holding the government to account.[6] This meant that the prorogation was voided, and the parliamentary session resumed.

Why does this matter? It matters because some constitutional scholars like Vernon Bogdanor defend the role of constitutional monarchy on the grounds that it guarantees the 'rules' of politics and ensures there is fair play in government and parliament.[7] We saw in the previous chapter that the whole purpose of constitutionalism is to provide a system of checks and balances, and to ensure the political system cannot be abused. But the fact that the Queen essentially *had to* accept Johnson's advice demonstrates that this definition of monarchy is a fantasy. Because it is a monarchy and therefore not electable, its power is derived from public will, which is tied to the government in power. The monarch cannot therefore be truly independent to ensure fair play, in a way that a president who is elected by the people can be. Indeed, the prorogation crisis demonstrated that the monarchy is essentially useless in its constitutional role, and moreover, it gives an *aura* of stability and protection, even if in reality there is no such thing. Despite widespread opposition from politicians, journalists and members of the public who staged a 'stop the coup' protest outside Westminster, the Queen could not use her constitutional rights to prevent Johnson's unlawful silencing of parliamentary democracy. Johnson's abuse of his powers to pursue a political agenda were left unchecked until the court's ruling.

In response to the crisis, the campaign group Republic argued that had a prime minister unlawfully advised an *elected* head of state, the head of state would have the authority to make a judgement if it was lawful or not before it went ahead.[8] And, if they were wrong in their judgement, they would have to take responsibility and resign. As it is, the Queen could not do either, and she instead became passive, subject to the whims of Johnson's Brexit agenda. Her passivity was further illustrated in much of the debate afterwards, which centred primarily on whether Johnson had 'lied' to the Queen in his advice.[9] This narrative makes Johnson the 'bad guy', while the Queen is depoliticized and absolved of responsibility. Even if it was true that Johnson knowingly falsified his advice (the court stopped short of ruling on the motives of the executive), this minimizes important questions about the monarch's role (or lack thereof) in ensuring political accountability. Rather than prompting debates about monarchy's usefulness to a contemporary democracy, the Queen instead became another victim of Johnson's moral bankruptcy, which put her on the side of 'the people' and therefore blameless. The potential harms of the monarch's non-power in comparison to an elected head of state were not addressed.

## Royal lobbying: the Queen and King's consent and the black spider memos

The Queen or King's consent – or Crown consent in Scotland – is a UK parliamentary convention whereby

Crown consent is required on proposed bills which would affect the Crown's prerogatives or interests. This includes 'the hereditary revenues, personal property or personal interests of the Crown, the Duchy of Lancaster, or … the Duchy of Cornwall'.[10] Prince's consent is also sought from the Prince of Wales on bills relating to the Duchy of Cornwall. Consent is usually sought early in the legislative process, before parliament can debate or vote on a bill. This is separate from the process of Royal Assent, which occurs when bills have passed in both Houses of Parliament and require Royal Assent to be declared Acts of Parliament. According to the role of constitutional monarchy, the monarch should only grant or withhold consent based on advice they receive from the government. In theory, then, consent is merely a formality.

The roles and purposes of consent are murky. A 2014 paper by the House of Commons Political and Constitutional Reform Committee which assessed the process of consent said 'the origins of Consent are unclear', although one account traces it to King George II giving consent to the Suppression of Piracy Bill in 1728.[11] It also commented that 'Consent is complex and arcane', with several pages in Erskine May (the guide to parliamentary practice) dedicated to when and how it should be sought.[12] This makes it very difficult for most citizens, and even some experts, to fully make sense of all of the requirements. Indeed, until recently, the procedure was almost entirely invisible. But in 2021, *The Guardian* launched an investigation into the (mis)uses of consent.[13] Using a database of

1,062 parliamentary bills that had been subject to the Queen's consent during Elizabeth II's reign, they found that the procedure was used far more widely than was believed. Consent was sought for bills including the Marriage (Same Sex Couples) Bill 2013 because it affected the legal rules for the Queen to give approval for some royal marriages, the Pensions Schemes Bill 2020, which would affect pension schemes for royal household employees, and the Counter-Terrorism and Security Bill 2015 because passports are issued under the royal prerogative. This demonstrates the huge range of bills that are subject to royal vetting. The stipulation that the bill must affect the Crown's prerogatives or interests suggests that it is only those bills that are *about* the Crown that would be inspected (for example, the Succession to the Crown Bill in 2013). But notions of what counts as affecting the Crown are opaque enough for many bills to count, giving the monarch remarkable access to the inner workings of government and parliament.

*The Guardian* also found that, although consent cannot be withheld without advice from the government to do so, royals seeing early versions of the bills meant that they could lobby for changes to draft legislation *before* giving their consent. They found multiple occasions where the Palace had requested changes, and it is not known how many others there are. This includes a transport bill in 1968, which was altered to mean that national traffic laws would not apply on the monarch's private estates,[14] and a 2021 Scottish bill that exempted the Queen's private lands from an initiative to cut carbon emissions by constructing new pipelines to heat buildings with renewable energy.[15] Prince Charles also used the Prince's consent to exempt his Duchy of Cornwall leasehold tenants from the right to buy their homes under the Leasehold Reform, Housing and Urban Development Act 1993 (see Chapter 7).[16] A Whitehall official said they agreed to the alterations to avoid 'a major row with the Prince of Wales'. In 2022, an internal Scottish government memo seen by *The Guardian* admitted 'it is almost certain some bills were changed before introduction to address concerns about crown consent'.[17] Constitutional law expert Thomas Adams said this evidenced 'the kind of influence over legislation that lobbyists would only dream of'.[18] Because consent is House procedure rather than a matter of statute, experts have said that it would be relatively easy for parliament to remove it without primary legislation.[19] However, despite the controversy of *The Guardian*'s investigation, no formal moves have been made to do so and the King and Prince's consent continues.

In a separate account of political lobbying, *The Guardian* submitted a series of Freedom of Information (FOI) requests to see correspondence between then-Prince Charles and government politicians and ministers (see Box 2.1). The 'black spider' memos – named for Charles's distinctive handwriting – were letters sent in a private capacity in which Charles expressed views and suggested action on a variety of issues, including herbal medicine, farming, the climate crisis and architecture. Many commentators defended the black spider memos as 'harmless' because they contain 'strong opinions but no political partisanship', and therefore do not directly challenge the political neutrality of the monarchy.[20] Similarly, in 2002 the Prince's office defended his right to 'private' correspondence with government ministers because 'it is proper and right that he should take an interest in British life'.[21] But there are two potential issues with these explanations. For one, writing directly to government ministers and having your letter read – never mind acted upon – is a privilege that most private citizens do not enjoy. Being able to lobby senior politicians, regardless of whether this is in a personal or royal capacity, is a position of significant power which should not be dismissed. There is some evidence of practice being amended in response to the memos; for example, in 2005 Tony Blair is said to have postponed implementation of new EU laws about selling herbal medicines, because the Prince had put Blair in touch with his contact at the Herbal Practitioners' Association, who argued that regulation was problematic.[22] Second, with the royals, the lines between 'private' and 'public' are inherently blurred. Charles is never 'just' a private citizen, because his entire being is tied up with his royal position (and, if he were 'just' a private citizen, why would a government minister care about his opinion anyway?). Therefore, regardless of whether his letters were politically or personally motivated, disclosing them is in the public interest because of his royal role.

## Box 2.1: The 'black spider memos'

It took *The Guardian* ten years of legal battles to have the black spider memos released. In 2010, the newspaper's initial FOI request was denied. It called for an FOI appeal tribunal, on the basis that the black spider memos were in the public interest, and according to the 'public interest test', any information like this (such as the spending of public money or misconduct in public office) must be released. While the tribunal was in process, the government made changes to tighten the FOI Act so that in the future the monarchy would be exempt from the 'public interest test'. Instead, the new rule was that royals could not be subject to FOI requests until 20 years after the creation of the record, or five years after their death, whichever was longer. *The Guardian* later found evidence that the monarchy had pressured government ministers to make the change.[23]

The results of the appeal were released in 2012, when the Administrative Appeals Chamber of the Upper Tribunal ruled that the letters should be published to ensure transparency for the public. This decision was vetoed a few weeks later by the Attorney General for England and Wales, the chief legal adviser to the sovereign and government, because it could damage the monarchy's political neutrality. In 2014, three Court of Appeal judges ruled that the Attorney General had 'no good reason' for using the ministerial veto. In 2015, the Supreme Court ruled that the Attorney General had acted unlawfully, and the letters were finally published.

In response to the scandal, the Campaign for Freedom of Information director Maurice Frankel said, 'The veto is not a trump card to be slipped out of a minister's sleeve to block any embarrassing disclosure'.[24]

The decade-long fight to release the black spider memos is illustrative of the extreme levels of secrecy around the monarchy, and the willingness of the Establishment to protect it. The Attorney General appears to have had little reason to employ the veto other than he disagreed with the legal decision. Additionally, the FOI Act was actively altered following the palace's lobbying over a decision they also disagreed with. The lengths to which those in power will go to protect the royals appears to have few bounds.

## Keeping secrets

There are varying tenors to these different forms of monarchical political lobbying and influence, but they come to the same end: that it is much vaster than commonly understood, opaque to the point that it is difficult to fully account for, and used in ways that are complex, unrecorded and constantly in flux. Because of the way the monarchy's political role has evolved over time, largely through precedent rather than constitutional record, the 'rules' outlined in the previous chapter do not necessarily function in practice.

Ultimately, this chapter has shown that what the monarchy promotes, facilitates and benefits from is *secrecy*, right at the heart of the British state.

The impenetrability of political procedures around monarchy's role mean that they can never be fully understood, nor fully accounted for. This is not just because they are unnecessarily complicated. Secrets are maintained 'through a combination of law, official practice, royal influence and a protective political culture'.[25] Despite the Freedom of Information Act listing all of the public authorities that are subject to it, the monarchy and the Royal Household are never mentioned, meaning they are essentially exempt from FOI requests.[26] Since a 1910 crisis in which George V's brother-in-law Prince Francis had bequeathed some royal jewels in his will to his lover, royal wills have been sealed so no one can discover what – and crucially, how much – is being inherited by whom.[27] This makes calculating the wealth of the royal family impossible, before we even get to the overly complicated and fractured ways that different public funds wind up in the palace (see Chapter 1).[28] And the National Archives, which usually make data available to everyone, has special prohibitions in place on Royal Archives and only gives a very small set of 'authorized' writers access to documents from the current reign.[29] One case saw a historian refused access to a Home Office file about police protection to the royal family between 1929 and 1939 because the regulator, the Information Commissioner, claimed 'there was a causal link between the disclosure of the requested information and the prejudice envisaged'.[30] An investigation by the Index on Censorship found that journalists and historians reported they had been unable to research the monarchy without conflict or difficulty, because archives had had materials removed, or there were gatekeepers actively restricting access.[31] In my own interviews with royal correspondents – journalists who report on the monarchy – they said that they would often get 'no comment' responses from the palace, and did not want to risk publishing something unconfirmed because this might mean the palace revokes their future access to royal news and events.[32]

Journalist Heather Brooke argues that secrecy and misinformation is central to systems of power in Britain, whereby keeping information hidden is one way in which the powerful can disclaim responsibility and, therefore, maintain their privilege.[33] The royals are able to achieve this to an astonishing extent. Historian Philip Murphy said that the monarchy's 'obsessive secrecy … impedes an informed and rational discussion about the nature of constitutional monarchy'.[34] It means that books such as this one, where we are seeking to understand what the monarchy is *for*, are very difficult to write because no one knows the full extent of the answer.

Brooke concludes her book by stating 'in a true democracy the state has no right to remain silent'.[35] Likewise, we might argue that if constitutional monarchy was running *as it is meant to run*, that is, as a system of checks and balances to ensure parliamentary procedure, then it would not need secrets. But the fact that the monarchy's political role is so difficult to explain demonstrates that perhaps everything is not working as it should. The 'rules' described in the previous chapter are occluded by other systems, whose central purpose seems to be to protect the role of hereditary monarchy and uphold existing systems of power and privilege. Moreover, as anthropologist Cris Shore argues, 'a monarch who both acts as head of state and is the embodiment of the state provides a potent and seductive way to mask that bureaucratic assemblage of governmental and executive powers that we call the state'.[36] They also do this, as we will now see, through various 'soft' and 'hidden' powers.

# PART II
# SOFT POWER

# 3

# THE GREAT UNIFIER?

Myth: 'The argument that the monarchy does not represent the will of the people is ludicrous. It is the most popular part of the UK government.'

Thomas Britton in *The Oxford Blue*, 2023[1]

When the British public were asked by BMG Research in 2023 what they most associate with notions of Britishness, the top three answers were the National Health Service (NHS), the monarchy and the Union Jack.[2] In a similar poll by YouGov about the 'best things about Britain', the monarchy was the fourth most popular answer, behind the NHS, Britain's countryside and Britain's history.[3] In a separate poll, YouGov found that 45 per cent of those surveyed – the majority response – said they were proud of the monarchy.[4]

These reports are unlikely to surprise you: we see them all the time. But what does it mean for the monarchy to be so tightly bound to ideas of national identity? Who, or what, is generating these narratives? Who is represented in these poll results and who is not? What is the monarchy for when it comes to national identity?

## Britain loves its monarchy

Let's start by considering the association between monarchy and national identity. There is no fixed connection between the nation and the state, and nations are 'socio-cultural and geographical constructs which ... have to be built'.[5] Creating a sense of nation entails ideological labour: continually renegotiating and redefining (imagined) national boundaries. Political scientist Benedict Anderson's theory of an 'imagined community' speaks to how nations are imagined by the people.[6] He argues that the evolution of the printing press from the 15th century onwards facilitated the production of mass news. This meant that rather than disparate local communities that shared local customs, people could start to share a national culture and language. This enabled a way of imagining being members of a broader collective of people, even though the vast majority of them would never actually meet.

Anderson's argument is that forms of media are a vital way through which nations are imagined into being. The monarchy is a good example of this. Again, most of us will never meet the monarch, nor even see them in real life. Rather, they circulate as a mediated image. For hundreds of years, coins stamped with the monarch's face would be how most people encountered them. Today, we see the monarch on television, in newspapers and online. All these examples create an imagined sense of nation. This is not accidental: it is purposefully constructed (see Figure 3.1).

It is through the repetition of images that monarchy and national identity come to be conflated. In the 1990s, social psychologist Michael Billig interviewed British families on their feelings towards the monarchy. One participant said, 'if you've not got the Royal Family there, then you'll not have the British Isles as we know it'.[7] This illustrates how the monarchy 'somehow embodies national identity [in a way that is] more or less ubiquitous ... self-evident, unproblematic and

**Figure 3.1: Union Flags lining the Mall to Buckingham Palace**

Union Flags, the national flag of the United Kingdom, line the Mall in London, the ceremonial route from Trafalgar Square to Buckingham Palace, the day before the wedding of Prince William and Kate Middleton, 28 April 2011.

"eternal"'.[8] It exists in a perpetual space, part of the status quo. In British schools, we learn the succession order of monarchs and a little rhyme to remember which of Henry VIII's wives he brutally murdered in a fit of misogynistic rage. To post a letter, we affix stamps featuring the monarch's portrait into a post box etched with the initials 'ER' or, now, 'CR', and they are collected by the *Royal* Mail. We have a post-work drink in the Crown (the second most popular pub name in the UK), the Royal Oak (the third most popular) or the Kings Arms (the ninth most popular).[9] These are part of a 'thick network of allusions to royalty in everyday life and popular culture' that means the presence of royalty is never far from our minds, even if unconsciously.[10] The key point here is that monarchy is not somehow inevitably and irrevocably a symbol of nation, rather, this is an association that has gradually accreted over time.

Monarchy and national identity are also evoked in more explicit ways, where monarchy is seen to contribute to national life. In popular discourse, one key defence of keeping the monarchy is that it is 'good for tourism', vaguely citing a supposed 'royal boost' to visitors during royal events.[11] For the Duke and Duchess of Cambridge's wedding in 2011, leading tourist organization VisitBritain claimed that the event would be 'great for tourism' and that the monarchy generates £500 million a year in tourism revenue.[12] Anti-monarchy campaigners Republic asked for proof of this claim, and found that VisitBritain had simply added up the ticket revenue of every single visitor to attractions with even the most tenuous connection to royalty, including St Paul's Cathedral. As Republic argue, visitors to St Paul's would most likely continue regardless of whether there is a monarchy or not. Even Buckingham Palace could feasibly continue as a tourist attraction if the monarchy were abolished. The Palace of Versailles has not been home to a reigning monarchy since Louis XVI left in 1789 (to be beheaded in 1793), and it welcomes about ten million visitors a year.[13] Like France, even if we abolished the monarchy tomorrow, monarchy would remain essential to our national history. Choosing to abolish the monarchy would change nothing about that history, but it could say everything about our national present and future.

The imagined associations between a current monarchy and national identity are not insignificant or inconsequential. If something is part of the status quo, we are less likely to question it, because it's seen to be almost beyond question. 'Monarchy is just there, it has always been there,[14] what difference does it make?' Earlier in this book, we debunked some of those notions that monarchy was 'powerless', or that it has no material consequences for Britain and the world. But these assumptions also matter in terms of what Britain is, or what Britain *thinks* it is. The survey respondents who say they are proud of the monarchy and what it represents are fans of more than just an odd Jubilee and Bank Holiday. As we'll see later in the book, the monarchy underpins systems of patriarchy, (neo)colonialism and inequality. If the monarchy is representative of Britain, then Britain is also patriarchal, (neo)colonialist and unequal. If we think the monarchy and the NHS are both things to be proud of, then we are comparing an institution which saves millions of lives each year despite having its funding cut to the bone, with an institution that has survived hundreds of years based on a belief in its own bloodline superiority. Monarchy is not an empty symbol, it shapes and is shaped by understandings of what Britain was, is and will be.

## What, or who, is this Britain that loves its monarchy?

The questions about people's feelings towards monarchy and national identity become even more interesting when we break them down by demographics. Let us return to that statistic that 45 per cent of Britons are proud of the monarchy and break it down by age. In fact, younger people were more likely not to be proud: 26 per cent said they were proud, 29 per cent were embarrassed and 32 per cent were neither. Comparatively, 64 per cent of older Britons said they were proud and 12 per cent said embarrassed. An earlier YouGov poll reported that between 2011 and 2022, 18–24 year olds became more conflicted about whether the monarchy should continue, going from 59 per cent approval in 2011 to 33 per cent in 2022.[15]

This significant decrease could be due to a number of factors: rising rates of societal inequality that mean the younger generation are much worse off than their parents, making it uncomfortable to witness royal privilege;[16] social media facilitating everyday forms of political engagement and protest, so young people constantly scroll through a plethora of political opinions; or just that the monarchy is seen as less representative of, and/or less relevant to, young British adults who live in a multicultural, globalized world. In 2011, we saw concerted attempts to represent royalty in a way that evoked renewal and modernization. Prince William and Kate Middleton's wedding played out as neoliberal meritocracy in action, as Kate Middleton – an 'ordinary' girl from a supposedly middle-class working family (despite her parents being multi-millionaires) – marries into an institution that is embracing the 21st century.[17] Fast forward to today, and Prince Andrew's alleged sexual abuse of minors and Prince Harry and Meghan Markle's experiences of racism and sexism depicted the monarchy as an obsolete institution not in keeping with the multicultural, global, post-#MeToo Britain that young people are experiencing.

It is revealing that although Meghan Markle's popularity has decreased in all age groups since 2018, she is still more popular with 18–24 year olds than with older demographics.[18] Like with Kate Middleton, around the time of Prince Harry and Meghan Markle's wedding many of the media reports spoke of progress and modernization. Markle was taken to represent multicultural Britain in an institution that has historically been very white. 'Harry and Meg's historic change for monarchy', cheered *The Sun*.[19] British journalist Lola Adesioye extolled, 'Black excellence in the royal family is a cool idea from a contemporary point of view', claiming that Markle's presence was a powerful message for women of colour.[20] Briefly, Markle made the monarchy seem more representative, and more in touch with an increasingly multicultural Britain.

As we now know, positive coverage of Markle quickly turned toxic. Racism against her and her children has demonstrated that supposed multicultural progress was impossible with Britain as it is.[21] It is perhaps not surprising, therefore, that approval for the monarchy is also lower among people of colour. British Future Think Tank found in 2022 that only 37 per cent of people from an ethnic minority wanted to retain the monarchy.[22] The same year, YouGov found that 38 per cent of ethnic minorities wanted to keep it, compared with 62 per cent of all Britons. Black Britons are much more likely to feel positively towards Meghan (63 per cent) and Harry (60 per cent) than the wider population (24 per cent and 29 per cent, respectively), although in the 65+ age bracket they have a significantly more negative view of the couple, suggesting an intersection of age and race.[23] Research has also found that people who migrated to or emigrated from the UK have difficulty incorporating the monarchy in their understandings of belonging and identity, because they do not see themselves represented in the 'traditional' version of national identity that the monarchy stands for.[24] While they may have favourable attitudes towards some individual royals (especially the late Queen), their views of the institution of monarchy were much more ambivalent, particularly after Brexit, which shifted their sense of belonging within a Britain that is increasingly isolationist.

The British monarchy is not only sovereign in the UK: 15 other countries share the monarch. These countries inevitably have even more complex relationships to it, and many accord it lower approval ratings. Indeed, some countries have announced they intend to vote on abolishing the monarchy (Antigua and Barbuda, Jamaica, Saint Vincent and the Grenadines, the Bahamas, Belize, Grenada, Saint Kitts and Nevis, and Saint Lucia), and Barbados became a republic in 2021. Because of the Crown's global reach, British national identity is not bounded. Many of these countries also have the 'thick network of allusions to royalty in everyday life', but with very different contextual implications.[25] Bridgetown in Barbados, for example, has multiple streets and locations named monarchically, such as Prince William Henry Street and Jubilee Gardens.[26] There has been much debate about whether to change these monikers upon achieving republican status because of their colonialist legacies.

Borders also matter within the UK. The devolved nations (Scotland, Wales and Northern Ireland) tend to have lower levels of support for monarchy. In Northern Ireland, the relationship is complex. Monarchism is central to unionists' political, social and religious identity: after the partition in 1921, the unionist government used royal visits to signify their belonging to the UK, and symbols of royalty were debated during the 1990s peace process, as unionists sought to retain them to differentiate themselves from the Republic.[27] Meanwhile Sinn Féin, the growing Irish republican party, dropped their original proposal to have a dual monarchy (Ireland and Great Britain having two separate governments but the same monarch) in 1917, to call for an Irish Republic.[28] YouGov data does not include Northern Ireland, but we can see the support for monarchy broken down for Great Britain.[29] In 2023, 62 per cent of people in England had a positive view of the royal family, compared to 56 per cent in Wales and just 43 per cent in Scotland. Meanwhile, 29 per cent of people in England had a negative view, versus 36 per cent in Wales and 51 per cent in Scotland (the figures also include 'don't know', which were 9 per cent each for England and Wales and 7 per cent for Scotland).

This is notable in the context of national identity, and seems to suggest that the monarchy represents a specifically *English* national identity (see Box 3.1), perhaps partly tied to Westminster politics. Scotland consistently shows the lowest approval ratings.[30] The unification of England and Scotland occurred in 1603 upon the succession of James VI of Scotland, who also became James I of England after Elizabeth I died childless. The Act of Union 1707 then merged Scotland and England into a single state of the United Kingdom of Great Britain, with a single parliament at Westminster.[31] As such, the UK is 'bundle of islands ... acquired at different times by the English crown'.[32] At Elizabeth II's coronation in 1953, this history prompted objections, as Scots protested the name 'Elizabeth II', considering Scotland never had an Elizabeth I. Protesters created merchandise celebrating the 1953 coronation of 'Elizabeth I', and others blew up mail boxes with the 'ER II' etching.[33] Today, some ministers in Scotland have suggested they might have a referendum on abolishing the monarchy if Scotland became independent. These anti-monarchy voices are not the majority, but it is certainly a louder voice than we see in English politics. One poll showed that most of those Scots asked viewed the monarchy as an 'English thing'.[34] A YouGov poll revealed that almost as many Scots want a republic (40 per cent) as want to keep the monarchy (46 per cent),[35] and a separate poll showed 41 per cent would keep the monarchy if Scotland became independent, as opposed to 40 per cent who would want an elected head of state.[36]

Political persuasion is important here, and the Scottish National Party, a centre-left party, is the largest political party by membership in Scotland. Perhaps unsurprisingly, left-wing voters are more likely to be anti-monarchy than right-wing ones.[37] Even so, there is still a remarkably small number of political stakeholders – left, right or anywhere in between – who publicly oppose the monarchy. (In)famously, former Labour Party leader Jeremy Corbyn was staunchly anti-monarchist (including allegedly refusing to kneel before the Queen when he was sworn in as a member of the Privy Council), and this was often used in the British tabloid media to discredit him, demonstrating again how monarchism is considered 'the norm' in national politics.[38] Interestingly, there was far more organized anti-monarchy activity in the 1970s–1990s, including Tony Benn's Commonwealth of Britain Bill, even though public feeling about abolition was much weaker. The lack of organized anti-monarchy advocacy in politics is not representative of much of the British and global population, nor of the diversity of subjects of the Crown in Britain and beyond.

### Box 3.1: Princes of Wales

In 1911, for the first time, Wales witnessed a ceremonial investiture of the Prince of Wales. Investitures had happened before, but usually in private in London or Westminster. This was the first time the investiture had evoked notions of Wales as a geographical space or 'Welshness' as an identity, connecting this to the Prince of Wales as a bridge between Wales and the British monarchy.

Historian John Ellis recounts how since the late 19th century, Wales had grown considerably in economic and political terms through things like the coal trade and shipping industry.[39] This meant that symbols of Welsh national identity, such as leeks, daffodils and dragons, were popularized by the Welsh as a way to exhibit their distinction from an English or even British national identity. An investiture of a Prince of Wales, therefore, was made to appeal to a distinctly Welsh identity. Prince Edward was presented to the people of Wales while the Welsh national anthem played, and symbols of Welsh nationality were embedded in the ceremony, such as the throne featuring dragons and daffodils. In 1969, the ceremony was repeated for the investiture of Prince Charles.

Why does this matter? The investiture of the Prince of Wales can be considered what historians Eric Hobsbawm and Terence Ranger term an 'invented tradition'.[40] These are practices that are presented as though traditional and having existed for centuries, but have actually been consciously created relatively recently to suggest historical legitimacy. They will often repurpose the trappings of traditionalism to do so; for example, the investiture used pseudo-medieval symbolism like swords. As Ellis argues, then, the investiture can be read as an attempt to address and reconcile social and cultural divisions between Wales and England, given that this was an extractive relationship at heart. It is a vehicle through which ethnicity, nationality and the state are redefined. The investiture does not flatten the national identities of the UK nations, but rather rewrites it in a way that makes monarchy an intrinsic part of the stories. The move attempts to make Wales feels represented in British national life and the establishment, and in so doing, perpetuates the unequal relationship between the two.

Prince Charles' investiture was met with controversy, including widespread protests about the existence of the Prince of Wales role in the first place and about the cost of the ceremony. In light of this, Prince William has said he will not have his own investiture ceremony to celebrate his inheritance of the title in 2022.[41]

## National identities

This chapter has addressed the multiple associations between monarchy and national identity. As we saw in the opening quote of this chapter, monarchy is often assumed to be for reproducing a coherent sense of nation: it is somehow inherently connected to national identity, and therefore should remain in power so as not to destabilize the nation. But this chapter has challenged that assumption. For one, we have discussed how national identity is itself a construct, forged and reforged in media and public culture. There is nothing inherent about the connection: it must constantly be reiterated to take hold. There is an ideological mission here. Indeed, over time, national identity could be rewritten to be *for* something else.

We have also thought about who 'Britain' is, and who is being represented. The 'Britain' characterized by an assumed monarchism excludes people who do not approve of the monarchy, where we find younger generations, people of colour, people who have migrated to or (to a lesser extent) emigrated from the UK, people living in the monarch's realms around the world, people who live in the UK's devolved nations, and left-wing voters over-represented. These are substantial populations, and their feelings towards the monarchy and inability to see themselves represented in a traditional, white, 'English', right-wing institution matters if we want to consider more inclusive visions of the nation. The monarchy is for ensuring a particular version of national identity is reproduced: and this version does not look like the nation.

# 4

# THE ULTIMATE CELEBRITIES?

Myth: 'The prince is a celebrity. Hereditary celebrity, and its opinion, is no more or less legitimate than that of a pop star, a sportsman, a novelist or Russell Brand, on all of whom the media dance attendance. Celebrity has influence only insofar as it commands public support. The rest is noise.'
Simon Jenkins, *Guardian* columnist, 2015[1]

Journalist Rosalind Coward famously referred to the monarchy in 1984 as '*The Royals*: the longest-running soap opera in Britain'.[2] *The Royals*, she argued, uses conventions of the family melodrama, with weddings, babies, break-ups and internal conflict. Because of this, she said, 'we never have to deal with the royal family as a political institution; we only have to think about human behaviour, human emotions, and choices restricted to the family'. More than 40 years later, the argument is still persuasive, although we may now refer to it as *Keeping up with the Windsors* as a nod to the behemoth reality show focusing on the lives of the elite, *Keeping up with the Kardashians*. We see the reality show at play in media reports which are far more interested in the brotherly rift between Princes William and Harry than revelations about the monarch's political meddling. Royals are just as likely to feature on the front page of *TMZ* as they are the *Daily Telegraph*. Princess Diana was the ultimate global icon, and the marriage between Prince Harry and actor Meghan Markle cemented the connection between monarchy and celebrity culture.

But the monarchy is not *equal to* celebrity, nor can it be straightforwardly equated to a soap opera or a reality show. Rather, as political theorist Tom Nairn wrote in his 1988 anti-monarchy polemic, while the royals 'have of course had to become celebrities in recent times, what really matters (and is really puzzling) about them is that they remain something more as well'.[3] To dismiss the royals as *just* celebrities, as Jenkins does in the opening quote, drastically oversimplifies the social, cultural, political and economic importance of monarchy that I outline in this book. It is perhaps more productive for us to consider celebrity culture and the entertainment industries as a *vehicle* for monarchy to reproduce itself in the public imagination, and the limits of this vehicle in terms of royal power.

## #WhereisKateMiddleton?

In 2024, the whereabouts of Kate Middleton caught the international imagination. In January, Kensington Palace announced she'd undergone 'abdominal surgery' and would be away from royal duties until Easter.[4] They made no further announcements, and by early March rumours and conspiracy theories had flooded social media.[5] A paparazzi photograph, supposedly of Kate and her mother Carole in a car, was claimed to not be her. Kensington Palace released a Mother's Day photograph of Kate and her children, which was sent to official news agencies for syndication. Social media users spotted errors in the image which suggested it had been significantly edited, and four photo agencies (AP, AFP, Reuters and PA) put out a rare 'kill notice' on the photo to remove it from its services, accusing the palace of digital 'manipulation'.[6] A tweet was later posted on Kate and William's official Twitter/X account, signed 'C' to indicate it came from Kate (Catherine), saying 'like many amateur photographers, I do occasionally experiment with editing'.[7] Soon afterwards, a video taken by the member of the public emerged of Kate and William at a farm shop, with social media users again claiming it wasn't her.[8] Rumours circulated about Kate being in a coma, having died, or pursuing a divorce from William. Finally, on 22 March, Kate announced in a video that she had been undergoing preventative treatment for cancer.[9]

#WhereisKateMiddleton, or #KateGate, tells us a lot about the royals' ever-changing relationship with the media. The story exploded partly due to the 24-hour news cycle; the rise of online misinformation; social media 'expertise' being almost indistinguishable from confirmed news stories; and the importance of 'clickbait' to online news funding models, which means that the more hyperbolic the headline, the more likely people are to open the link. Even as someone who has followed royal news for many years and spotted patterns in how royal news works, I struggled to make sense of what was 'real'. The online frenzy then permeated the mainstream media. On CBS primetime *The Late Show with Stephen Colbert*, Colbert publicly claimed that Kate's 'disappearance' was linked to William's alleged extramarital affairs.[10] Rumours of his alleged affairs have been reasonably commonplace on social media for many years, but have largely remained unacknowledged in mainstream media. #KateGate seemed to break new ground around what people felt was now acceptable to say about the royals.

Much of the commentary came from the United States, a country with a very different relationship to the royal family because the institution has no political significance there. US media has long held an interest in the monarchy – during Queen Victoria's reign, American newspapers reported on the moustache style of her husband, Prince Albert.[11] Princess Diana's death echoed familiar narratives of glamorous celebrities who died in tragic circumstances at relatively young ages, like Grace Kelly or James Dean, who also died following car crashes and have since been turned into icons of the Hollywood golden age. Diana also parlayed with American celebrity, for example, in the iconic image of her dancing with actor John Travolta at the White House (see Figure 4.1). She featured on the cover of *People* magazine – an American celebrity gossip publication – 58 times, more than any other

**Figure 4.1: Princess Diana dancing with John Travolta at the White House**

The iconic photograph of Princess Diana dancing with actor John Travolta at the White House, which affirmed Diana's place in Hollywood, 9 November 1985.

person in its history.[12] Her humanitarian commitment set out a template for the philanthropy often enacted by Hollywood movie stars and pop stars today, as publicly being seen to 'give back' has become essential to celebrity branding and notions of authenticity. The marriage of Prince Harry and Meghan Markle further shifted the picture. Her pre-existing celebrity profile, their decision to leave the royal family, relocate to California, undertake tell-all confessional interviews with the 'Queen of Hollywood' Oprah Winfrey, and Harry's autobiography have further blurred the lines between royalty and the contemporary celebrity industries (see also Box 4.1).

Back in the UK, Harry and Meghan's revealing accounts of royal life have prompted audiences to expect more transparency from the monarchy than before. The Palace's approach to announcing Kate's absence from royal duties – to release just one statement saying she was undergoing surgery and would not be seen until after Easter – is entirely in keeping with monarchy's approach to public relations. They say very little and are very discreet with what information they do release. In my research interviews with royal correspondents, many exhibited exasperation at how little the royal Communications Offices actually told them, with their preferred response to journalists being 'no comment'. As one royal correspondent said to me, this 'frustrat[es] the journalistic process'.[13] Likewise, very little access is permitted to the royals themselves. Over her seven-decade reign, despite being the most represented person in history, Elizabeth II never gave an in-depth media interview.[14] We never knew her personal opinions on most things (except horses and dogs): she existed almost exclusively as an image and an icon. The tactic of saying very little has worked for the royals for many years, but with expanding media technologies, this is becoming harder to maintain. We saw the challenges of this emerging in 1997 with the initial handling of Diana's death. At first, the Queen stayed silent, and remained in Balmoral Castle in Scotland rather than returning to London. The outpouring of public grief for Diana prompted accusations that the Queen had not responded appropriately: she was not representing the public, who wanted a cipher through which to channel their grief. In a rare moment of criticism of the Queen, the *Daily Express* published the headline, 'Show us you care: mourners call for the Queen to lead our grief'.[15] This led to the Queen returning to Buckingham Palace and making a televised tribute to Diana. The age of social media, with constant news cycles and social media punditry, has made monarchy's media relations even more complex. This is a sign of the future challenges the monarchy faces.

### Box 4.1: The rise of Queen Camilla

The rise of Queen Camilla is an interesting case for us to consider the similarities and differences between the monarchy and the celebrity industries, where in both cases, public relations is key.

Charles and Camilla's affair became public knowledge upon the 1992 publication of *Diana: Her True Story*, an authorized biography by Andrew Morton, in which Diana accused Charles of infidelity. In 1993 this was followed by the leaking of an intimate sexual conversation between Charles and Camilla, which had been secretly recorded.

In 1997, around the time of Diana's death, the BBC conducted opinion polls that suggested two-thirds of British people didn't want Charles to become king if he married Camilla, and 86 per cent thought that Camilla shouldn't be queen.[16]

The same year, Charles hired Mark Bolland, a public relations executive, to rehabilitate the public image of Camilla and of their relationship.[17] She began by accompanying Charles to some public events, before they were photographed together in what appeared to be a staged paparazzi shot at the Ritz Hotel in London. In 2001, she became president of the Royal Osteoporosis Society, and then later attended the Golden Jubilee celebrations in 2002, where she was filmed in the royal box behind the Queen, which ensconced her within the royal public service model (see Chapter 5). They married in 2005, and by 2015, 53 per cent of British people thought she should be queen consort.[18] As we now know, at Charles's coronation in 2023, Camilla was crowned not queen consort but queen, seemingly demonstrating the overwhelming success of Bolland's plan.

The rehabilitation of Camilla shows how the monarchy makes use of media culture. The rewriting of the narrative took decades, but through slowly presenting her in a favourable light, Bolland was able to largely associate Camilla with the markers of royalty, such as charity work and public events. One distinctiveness of royalty versus celebrity is that royals can play the long game. While celebrity is often ephemeral, monarchy is unlikely to disappear overnight, so it has the time to stage its public relations over longer periods of time (without rushing to post a public apology from the iPhone Notes app, à la Justin Bieber and co.).

## Staging ordinariness

According to academic Chris Rojek, there are three types of celebrity status: ascribed (famous because of their lineage); achieved (famous because of their skill or talent); and attributed (famous because they attract a lot of media attention). The royal family sit in the ascribed category, because their position is inherited. New members of the royal family automatically become celebrities by virtue of their position. Rojek goes on to discuss the changing relationship between celebrity and monarchy:

> As modern society developed, celebrities have filled the absence created by the decay in the popular belief in the divine right of kings, and the death of God. The American revolution sought to overthrow not merely the institutions of colonialism but the ideology of monarchical power too. It replaced them with an alternative ideology ... the ideology of the common man. ... Celebrities replaced the monarchy as the new symbols of recognition and belonging.[19]

This description speaks to our changing relationship to systems of power, as we discussed in the Introduction. 'Power' is no longer conceived as 'top down' from a king or a god; rather it is disciplinary, operating throughout society.

We can see this power in action in changing media representations of the royal family. Consider portraits of historical monarchs. In 'The Armada Portrait' of Elizabeth I (c. 1588) (further discussed in Chapter 8), Elizabeth I rests her hand atop a globe to represent

England's imperial power in the Americas while Spanish Armada ships founder in the sea behind her, and fine clothing and opulent surroundings symbolize her class privilege. Such images of global dominance and military strength worked to position the monarchy at the top of a strict classed and racialized hierarchy, where only the white upper classes had power and influence. Everyone must know their place. Under Victoria, royals started to reflect the values of the bourgeois family, and today, representations of the royal family draw much more on the tenets of celebrity culture, or as Rojek calls it, 'the ideology of the common man'. Photographs we see of Kate and William's children, for example, are much more relaxed and informal, often featuring them playing outside or being dropped off at school by their parents. They are behaving 'just like us'. This evokes ordinariness, as the royals perform 'relatability' to distance them from accusations of privilege and make them appear closer to the public.

Celebrity culture often plays with ideas of ordinariness buried beneath extraordinariness. Celebrities are positioned as inherently special, otherwise they wouldn't be notable. We must believe they deserve their privileged position. Conversely, confessional interviews, behind-the-scenes footage and home photoshoots all cultivate intimacy and relatability between a celebrity and their fans. Balancing the two is essential to any celebrity narrative, as we must simultaneously believe they are exceptional *and* that we can relate to them.[20] Careful equilibrium is perhaps even more vital for the royals, whose special position in society upholds the entire monarchical institution. If royalty becomes too ordinary, the status of the institution and its connections to the state, government, nationalism and religion are at risk. Monarchy's use of celebrity culture, then, must be careful and strategic. If we had started hearing about how the Queen hated particular prime ministers, or how tedious she found waving on the Buckingham Palace balcony, her revered status would have been fractured.

Balancing celebrity and royal presentations of ordinariness and extraordinariness are made more challenging with developing media technologies, which facilitate our access. This is a deliberation that royal officials were having very publicly in 1952. Plans for the Queen's coronation were under way, and some people at the BBC and the *Daily Express* wanted it to be aired on live television. The *Daily Express* said it would invest the monarchy with 'a new kind of legitimacy' if the public felt like they were an intimate part of the coronation celebrations.[21] Live television was very new at the time, and many people saw it as indicative of the dumbing down of popular culture. This was not theatre or opera: it was low-brow, tasteless entertainment for the masses. Media theorists have since debunked such classed hierarchies and argued that *all* media is culture.[22] But organizers of the coronation had serious concerns that television would be dangerous for the monarchy. People might eat during the Queen's coronation oath! People might talk over a prayer! You can't control how people engage with something when it's beamed directly into their homes.

They ended up with a compromise, whereby the coronation was broadcast live, but the most religious elements (like the anointing) were not shown. There were many debates over showing close-ups of the Queen's face, because such voyeurism was seen as invasive, and again this was compromised on by agreeing that all close-ups would be discreet and only of particular moments.[23] This ensured a balance between the ordinary and the extraordinary: people were given access to the event, but only on specific terms. The broadcast ended up being a great success. Just as the *Daily Express* had expected, television allowed people to see their ruler and feel connection to the institution. Media culture was a vehicle through which people's affinity to the institution was reproduced.

Other royal representations have shown what happens when things *don't* go so well, or when the balance is thrown off. In 1987, the BBC aired *It's a Royal Knockout*, based on slapstick television gameshow *It's a Knockout*, which featured people undertaking comical games in fancy dress. *It's a Royal Knockout* featured Princes Andrew and Edward, Princess Anne and Sarah Ferguson (Prince Andrew's then-wife) captaining celebrity teams dressed in Tudor costumes. It was widely criticized, because it 'gave the impression of the Royal Family using their privileged access to the media to sell themselves',[24] and evidenced 'the irruption of showbiz into the royal world'.[25] The royals had become too ordinary, and the extraordinariness of the institution was under threat.

There is some irony here in this idea of the monarchy using 'the media to sell themselves'. Critics of *It's a Royal Knockout* thought it was crude for the royals to be promoting themselves like other celebrities do. But both *It's a Royal Knockout* and coronations of monarchs are choreographed public relations exercises to reproduce an institution in the public imagination, albeit in very different forms. In May 2023, television scriptwriter Gareth Roberts channelled the debates of the 1950s in an opinion piece for *The Spectator* entitled 'Monarchy and celebrities should not mix'. In it, he argued that the list of celebrity guests at Charles III's coronation – which included David and Victoria Beckham, TV presenters Ant and Dec, and pop star Katy Perry – was indicative of 'a shaky feeling of decline' of the monarchy, whereby the religious significance of the coronation was lost and it became mere popular entertainment. There is more than a whiff of class prejudice in Roberts' piece, as he contrasts the 'sacred rite' of the coronation with celebrity culture: at one point he sarcastically suggests they 'get Gemma Collins down', referring to the former star of ITV reality series *The Only Way is Essex* as, apparently, the tawdry antithesis of monarchy. We've seen this kind of attitude before: consider people's snide responses to Meghan Markle being a 'briefcase girl' on gameshow *Deal or No Deal*, and how it was somehow unbefitting of a royal. Why are Gemma Collins and the royals seen to be so different? They both use PR to promote their brand. They both rely on different forms of media culture so people know about them, thereby enabling them to have a career. They both 'influence' people, for example, the clothes worn by Kate Middleton often immediately sell out. People who sniff at Gemma Collins for crude self-promotion should reconsider what royal coronations and weddings are really for: at their essence, they promote the royal brand. The perceived difference is that the royals must be seen as above such tawdry promotion, and by doing it they are drawing attention to the fact that they're not that different. They are tarnishing the monarchy's mystique.

## Celebrity and so much more

In the popular US imagination, celebrity and royalty are conflated. One way we can explain this is by considering geographical models of wealth and fame, in which the Hollywood system mirrors broader ideologies of the 'American dream'. In this context, celebrity becomes an avatar of social mobility and meritocracy, where anyone can make it if they work hard enough. While the American dream has translated across borders as a global shorthand for social mobility, royal celebrity means something different elsewhere. In the UK, for example, the royals do not exist purely within entertainment culture, but have attachments to aristocratic and political power that comprise an elite and exceptional category of British celebrity. They therefore operate on a different register to even the most unique British celebrities, including those informally designated as 'national treasures'.[26] There is something culturally specific about how royal celebrity is wielded, and hence in what it *means*. To say that the monarchy is merely for entertainment, like Jenkins in the opening of this chapter, significantly undermines the importance and influence of it as a political institution. Indeed, this acts as a distraction to the important constitutional functions of monarchy, and its wealth, power and privilege, which far surpasses any other celebrity.

However, it is useful to consider celebrity culture as a *vehicle* for the continuation of royal power. Monarchy's use of celebrity culture is strategic, to ensure its visibility (and therefore relevance) in the public imagination. We shouldn't entirely dismiss royal celebrity, then, but rather scrutinize its (soft) power.

# 5
# PUBLIC SERVANTS?

> Myth: 'My family have not done this because it looks
> good – they do it because charity is not an optional
> extra in society ... we believe that, above anything else,
> charities nurture, repair, build and sustain our society.
> Without the work that charities do, society would be an
> empty shell.'
>
> Prince William, 2018[1]

Since the 19th century, the monarchy has carefully
honed its image as an institution that exists in service
of the public and the public good, with charitable
activities, introduced by Queen Victoria, constituting
the bulk of what is called royal 'work'.[2] The phrase
'full-time working royal' is used to describe those
who do not pursue other careers and spend their time
representing the monarch. Such framing uses soft
power to give the royals, and therefore the monarchy,
place and purpose: they are productive members of
civil society.

'Public service' implies serving the public good. Prime ministers and members of parliament (MPs) are said to be undertaking public service. Their intended role is to act as representatives of the people, reflect the public voice and represent the national interest. We might also think of public services, things like healthcare or waste management that keep society functioning. We may or may not agree that all MPs or all public services fulfil the values of selflessness or serving the public good. But the point is that to call something a public service evokes those notions, and it suggests that something has a critical social function.

This chapter will unpack the meaning of royal work and public service, which is often presented as the monarchy's key role in society. This encompasses many activities: the royals act as patron or president to over 3,000 organizations,[3] including various regiments in the armed forces; undertake visits, cut ribbons or unveil plaques for organizations and services; host garden parties at Buckingham Palace for people who have 'made a positive impact in their community';[4] and preside over the honours system. Each of these frames the institution as benevolent or paternalistic: serving others, 'giving back' and undertaking social good.

## What is royal public service?

In the book *Royal Bounty*, Frank Prochaska describes the history of royal charitable and social work, and the shaping of what he calls 'the welfare monarchy'.[5] He argues that prior to the 17th and 18th centuries, monarchs reigned under the divine right of kings: a political doctrine that decreed monarchs were appointed by God. Any direct contact between the monarch and the people was based on the premise that the monarch was sacred. This included the aforementioned royal touch, a belief that monarchs could heal the sick through touch (see Figure 5.1); royal maundy, where monarchs distributed silver coins to the elderly; patronages of hospitals (which were then voluntary, funded by donations); and donating money to the poor. By the reign of George III (1760–1820), royal authority was increasingly reinforced through a type of 'popular paternalism' that demonstrated sympathy with the working and middle classes.[6] Socio-politically, philanthropy had

Figure 5.1: 'Queen Anne touching Dr Johnson, when a boy, to cure him of Scrofula or the "King's Evil"', artist unknown, 18th century

become a key social value in Victorian Britain, with religious doctrines of 'helping others' and 'duty' representing enlightenment.[7] Queen Victoria visited hospitals, working-class cottagers and armed forces personnel, while Prince Albert focused on housing conditions for the poor. The First and Second World Wars gave royals new opportunities to perform public duty. Princess Elizabeth famously joined the Auxiliary Territorial Service in 1945, the Princess Royal visited war canteens, the Duke of Kent visited bomb sites and Queen Mary met evacuees. Royals have since extended their work with the military, for example, Prince Harry's founding of the Invictus Games for wounded soldiers.[8]

Service and duty were part of a carefully curated persona developed over Elizabeth II's life, from her 1947 speech in which she declared 'my whole life, whether it be long or short, shall be devoted to your service',[9] to many obituaries which referred to her as 'the ultimate public servant'.[10] *Forbes* wrote, 'the Queen was a lady deeply committed to public service and her sense of duty was unwavering, even astounding'.[11] A 2021 YouGov survey found that some respondents named the Queen their hero and a 'role model', with those same people saying that the qualities of a hero were 'acting selflessly and to benefit others'.[12] This is a complete pivot from the divine right of kings, which rested on the assumption of innate superiority.

Opening hospitals or hosting charity parties might constitute the day-to-day activities of royals, which makes them appear as forms of work. But, taking

Prochaska's history, these are acts that have *become* royal activities over time, as ideological tools to reposition the monarchy in the public imagination. Tobias Harper's history of the honours system is a further demonstration of how this works.[13] Twice a year since 1888, the British government has published a list of people who have been awarded state honours, and since 1948 these are presented at an investiture by the monarch or a senior royal (another 'invented tradition' – see Chapter 4). Before 1993, people were awarded for different services to the state, the nation and the empire. The system was then reformed and 'volunteer work' was explicitly given priority. Harper suggests this had a symbiotic effect, whereby the morality of the monarchy and its leadership of the voluntary sector were boosted by the credibility of the honours system, and vice versa. Royal work works both ways.

## Morality and elite philanthropy

The official royal website claims that 'Royal patronages add status to an organisation, and visits and involvement from a Royal Patron can often bring much-needed publicity'.[14] This is not exclusive to royals: celebrities, for example, can also boost charities' profiles and bring valuable visibility. But in 2020, a report by charity consultancy Giving Evidence found that 74 per cent of charities with a royal patron had not received any public engagements from their patron in the previous year. They also found that there was no evidence that royal patrons increase a charity's fundraising, revenue or the generosity of the public.[15] Moreover, charities are not the only potential beneficiary in this arrangement. Being seen to be undertaking 'social good' is a huge boost for public figures, as it improves their image.

Scholars have coined the term 'philanthrocapitalism' to explain how elites use philanthropy to legitimize their wealth.[16] Elites are seen to be 'giving something back', and their wealth is acceptable because they are 'doing something good' with it.[17] Classic social theorists like Pierre Bourdieu have explored the social and economic functions of gift-giving.[18] The central argument is around the logic of exchange. That is, while gift-giving may appear altruistic, in fact there are social expectations that the gift will be reciprocated in some way. This might be that if you give a gift to a friend on their birthday, you expect one in return when yours comes around. It might also be that if elites undertake philanthropy and give the gift of money, or time, then they expect to be recompensed. This doesn't mean that they will receive financial recompense, but rather that their act will benefit them in some way, by, for example, creating positive public opinion around them. This is a form of soft power, shaping public responses to elite wealth by attaching it to notions of morality and respectability. Royal philanthropy operates similarly. As society's interests and values change, so too does the monarchy. It adapts and remakes itself in the image of a shifting moral economy, performing public duty in return for its continued privilege and power.

Philanthrocapitalism and inequality do not exist independently, but are rather intimately intertwined.[19] Critics of philanthrocapitalism point out that, first, if the world was a more equal place, we might not need as much charity to begin with, and, second, if elites gave away more of their wealth, they might be able to contribute towards creating that more equal world. If the point of philanthropic work is for it to ensure the current social system, then it cannot hope to fight for social justice.

## The Big Help Out

The Big Help Out was a key initiative in the programme of events scheduled for King Charles' coronation in May 2023. The official royal website claims that the event encourages people to volunteer in their local communities and help others 'in tribute to His Majesty the King's public service'.[20] The aim was to get as many people as possible taking part in voluntary work on a single day.

The Big Help Out came a few weeks after the National Council for Voluntary Organisations report found that volunteering is at an historic low in England, down by about 50 per cent since the COVID-19 pandemic.[21] The framing of the Big Help Out suggests that if individuals would just make more effort to volunteer, then the voluntary sector would be replenished and fewer people in need would suffer. This entirely depoliticizes the crisis the UK finds itself in. The dip in volunteering occurred during a cost-of-living crisis, in which more and more people struggle to pay bills and afford basic necessities like food and heat. This leaves people less emotionally, physically or mentally able to volunteer their time to help others. Moreover, the cost-of-living crisis did not just appear. It is the direct result of decisions made by successive Conservative governments to cut public services, pursue Brexit, which was one path to inflation, protect the rights of landlords in the private rented sector, and not build enough affordable housing. While volunteers can (and do) make extremely valuable differences to individuals, they cannot address the systemic inequalities that cause the issues in the first place. The Big Help Out makes no reference to these issues, and by focusing on the role of individuals rather than the wider political system, it leaves deep inequalities intact. Therefore, the Big Help Out mirrors the rest of royal public service, presenting a depoliticized model of civic duty. The monarchy would not want to dismantle the wider political system, because systems of inequality benefit it. It does not want systemic changes, because these changes might just mean the monarchical institution is abolished in favour of something that does not enshrine privilege.

There are also inequalities in how wealth is distributed. The final cost of the coronation has still not been made public (which is telling given the economic scrutiny applied to public institutions like the National Health Service [NHS]), but was estimated to cost between £50 and £100 million, the majority of which came from public funds.[22] We should also remind ourselves that the UK is the last country in Europe to host a full-scale coronation; other states now have much simpler ceremonies. Meanwhile, Sure Start, a child-focused initiative which provides childcare, health support and community development, has seen 1,416 of its centres close since 2010 because of government cuts.[23] If the coronation funding had been diverted, many more children could be protected.

Some charity owners interviewed by *The Guardian* said that the Big Help Out's association with the monarchy made them feel unable to taking part. As Quamina, founder of Dope Black Queers, put it, 'the monarchy is the very antithesis of what my charity is about – many of the difficulties we face in society are a direct result of colonialism and the monarchy, both historically and how they operate now'.[24] Quamina makes an important point. One of the issues with philanthrocapitalism, as social scientists have argued, is that it absolves the state of taking responsibility for the citizenry. That is, if civil society comes in to patch up the gaps left by government funding cuts, it is no longer considered the government's problem to fix it. This is a neoliberal model of governance, whereby the government can effectively step back and let individuals care for one another. The more this happens, the more they can cut. The 'care crisis' refers to how health and social care systems have been starved of funding, and largely rely on the goodwill of workers to, for example, remain in work unpaid for hours after their shift has ended because no one will arrive to take over.[25] But eventually over time the goodwill is eroded. Between 2018 and 2022 43,000 people aged 21 to 50 left the Nursing and Midwifery Council register.[26] It is a similar picture for childcare, disability, housing and elderly care services. They cannot rely entirely on voluntary labour, because these are essential services which require training and skills that need to be fairly remunerated. Positioning vocations like nursing as a 'public service' mean that they become framed as a 'calling', paid for through social capital rather than a fair wage and decent working conditions. Likewise, care services' proximity to the voluntary sector, bolstered by the royals, means that calls for the government to fairly fund the services can be rebuffed. Thousands of NHS workers were invited to sit in a special grandstand outside Buckingham Palace to celebrate Charles' coronation in May 2023, which culture secretary Lucy Frazer said was 'a mark of the nation's profound gratitude' to the health service. But the invitation came at the same time as NHS staff went on strike because the government had refused to negotiate with them over fairer wages.[27] The invitation therefore seems like a hollow, symbolic 'celebration' of health workers' public service, while their work is repeatedly devalued by those who *do* have the power to reward them materially. Royal public service and philanthropy are not only upholding monarchy's power, but also the broader systems and structures of inequality that render the poorest in society worst off (see Box 5.1).

## Box 5.1: Diana, the 'people's princess'

Princess Diana is often remembered for her global charity work. Her causes included campaigning against landmines, and visiting HIV/AIDS and leprosy clinics where she was famously seen shaking hands with patients, helping to dispel stigma that the viruses were spread through hand contact.

Diana's charity work adds an important dimension to this chapter. The global dimension of her philanthropy shifts the debate, as while royal public service in the UK reproduces national inequalities and absolves the state of responsibility, Diana's projected a 'politics of transnational pity and love'.[28] That is, rather than addressing the structural roots of global inequalities that might be attributed to colonialism, war, ecology, global value chains and so on, it individualizes struggle to romanticize the morality of the Global North in showing compassion for those less fortunate. In turn, it depoliticizes the struggles of the Global South, so that geopolitics are seen as merely the result of good or bad luck.

Biographies of Tony Blair, Labour Prime Minister from 1997 to 2007, show that until her death three months after he came to power, Blair had had multiple discussions with Diana about her becoming a global ambassador for Britain. As scholar Raka Shome argues, Diana's 'global image of compassion and sensitivity' was in line with Blair's New Labour government's vision of globalization and modernization.[29] Shome goes on to suggest that Diana was often positioned as a 'global mother', and a partnership between her and New Labour would position Britain in line with Commonwealth logics that Britain is the head of a 'family of nations'. Here, the 'global mother' is the white mother, reproducing global norms around gender, race, sex and nationhood. Although Diana was, at the time, operating as a relative outsider to the monarchy, given that she had divorced Charles, her position as 'the people's princess' and as the future king's mother ensured she remained symbolically royal. We can also see that Diana's compassion is now evoked in representations of her two sons' approach to charity work, which is much more emotionally engaged than, for example, that of Charles. Their Heads Together charity (now headed by William and Kate) for mental health focuses on emotional intelligence and 'talking therapy', which reflects Diana's 'touchy-feely' approach, but again does not address the deeper causes, suggesting that problems can be 'talked away' rather than being addressed systemically.

## Royal trickle-down economics?

Despite what Prince William claimed in the opening quote of this chapter, public service has an important ideological function for monarchy. It is a form of soft power that diverts attention away from royal wealth and privilege, and instead repackages the royals as selfless servants of the people. Monarchy becomes symbolic of the voluntary sector and the power of caring for others, even while it continues to extract capital and value, and indeed, even while it shores up the very systems that are causing inequalities in the first place. No monarchy can fight for social justice, because social justice is antithetical to its very existence. No amount of charity work will 'give back' the amount of wealth the monarchy takes: there is no such thing as royal 'trickle-down economics'. The very purpose of monarchy is to hoard, to take and to exploit.

# PART III
# HIDDEN POWER

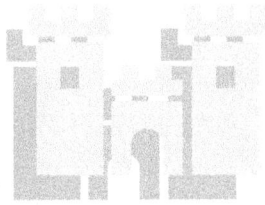

# 6
# POST-COLONIAL?

Myth: 'Several commentators, mostly in America and some of them academics, have seen fit to pour insults on the late Queen. As well as their sheer nastiness, they display their ignorance: she was central not to colonialism, but to successful and largely peaceful decolonization and the creation of a Commonwealth of equals.'

Ben Domenech in *History Reclaimed, 2022*[1]

In March 2022, William and Kate were on a state visit to the Caribbean. State visits usually consist of royals greeting members of the public, visiting local organizations and charities, and attending formal events with state officials. They are followed on these visits by a select group of media organizations, who document it for the UK and international media.[2] Ordinarily, the footage will feature choreographed images portraying the royals as friendly, philanthropic and interested in global issues.

The standout photograph of this tour was less positive. In Jamaica, William and Kate stood on one side of a six-foot metal fence, flanked by suited bodyguards. On the other side, Jamaican children poked their fingers through the fence to try and reach the royals, who smile, wave and occasionally shake their hands. The photograph has been well circulated in global media and in public commentary as being 'tone deaf'[3] and a 'throwback to colonialism',[4] given the wire fence separating the children of colour from the royals, and the history of Jamaica as a British colony. It was especially controversial considering that many nations around the world – including Jamaica itself – are debating removing the British monarch as their head of state because of its associations with empire. Indeed, neighbouring Barbados became a republic in 2021. The photograph also appeared against the backdrop of Black Lives Matter, a global movement which drew attention to colonialism and racial oppression, and prompted global calls for reparations for the slave trades.

While this photograph is one of the more explicit representations of the monarchy's colonial power, in this chapter we will speak back to Domenech's claim about decolonization, and discuss how state visits, the presence of a British monarch as head of state overseas, and the Commonwealth, demonstrate that, in fact, coloniality persists. I use the word coloniality in this chapter as distinct from colonialism. Coloniality refers to the colonial patterns of thought and power structures that emerged as a result of colonialism, and continue to define politics, economics, cultures and societies today. Coloniality shapes forms of knowledge and practice. In many ways coloniality and the monarchy are indivisible, given that the presence of the monarchy internationally evokes empire and whiteness. To begin, let's document the history of empire and monarchy.

## The Empress of India

The establishment, expansion and preservation of the British empire and the transatlantic slave trade can be attributed to a series of British monarchs, beginning in the Tudor age. In 1532, Henry VIII declared that England was an empire as part of the Ecclesiastical Appeals Act, which was his attempt at breaking away from Rome by declaring the crown imperial. His daughter, Elizabeth I, granted a Royal Charter for exploration to soldier Humphrey Gilbert in 1578, who used it to establish a colony in Newfoundland, Canada. In 1562, naval commander John Hawkins became the first known English person to profit from the 'triangular trade', selling enslaved people from Africa to Spanish colonies in the West Indies. This was so lucrative that Hawkins asked Elizabeth I to fund his second slave voyage, and members of her royal court became investors. The Queen loaned Hawkins one of her ships for the voyage and gave permission for it to fly her flag, the royal standard. On this trip, he took over 400 enslaved people from Africa to the Americas.[5]

Elizabeth I also granted a charter to the British East India Company as a joint-stock company in 1600, to trade in the Indian Ocean region and later East Asia. Using an army of 260,000 soldiers at its peak in 1803, twice the size of the British standing army at that time, the company colonized large parts of the Indian subcontinent, Southeast Asia and Hong Kong, and by 1750 the company accounted for half the world's trade in commodities including cotton, sugar, spices, tea, silk and opium. The company eventually assumed administrative functions and ruled over large areas of India, before the Government of India Act 1858 signed control of India over to the British Crown. The company rose to power through extreme violence, torture, murder and pillaging of local communities in a relentless pursuit of profit and power. It also established the business model (stakeholders, for example) upon which much corporate ownership rests today, where global conglomerates are also wreaking their own version of neocolonialism by exploiting communities for profit.[6]

In documents pertaining to the slave-trading South Sea Company, another British joint-stock company founded in 1711, historian Nicholas Radburn found an illustration of a crown resembling the St Edward's headpiece used in British monarch's coronations. The accompanying text said that this was 'the Mark henceforward, to be put upon the Bodys of the Negros to be sold & Dipos'd of in the Spanish West Indies', under a contract between Britain's Queen Anne and Spain's King Philip V.[7] According to this, then, enslaved people's bodies were branded with the mark of the British crown as a sign of ownership and power.

Historian Camilla de Koning has also found documents that showed Queen Anne's diplomacy skills were central to Britain being given a contract from Spain to transport 4,800 Africans per year to the Spanish colonies.[8] After the success of the East India Company, Charles II formed the Royal African Company in 1660, led by the Duke of York, who would later become James II. The Royal African Company was given a monopoly over all trade with Africa, extracting gold and ivory from the Gold Coast. Its biggest commodity, however, was the transportation of slaves, and historians have estimated that the Royal African Company shipped more enslaved African people – approximately 150,000 of them – to the Americas than any other company during the Atlantic slave trade.[9] As king, James II continued to be the company's chief stockholder.[10] These examples show that connections between monarchy, colonialism and slavery were not just policy-driven, nor merely symbolic; monarchs were materially and economically invested in, and therefore complicit with, empire's violence.[11]

Queen Victoria assumed the title of Empress of India in 1877 to bind India more closely to Britain's crown control, and by 1920 'the empire upon which the sun never sets' was 13.71 million square miles.[12] Portraits of Victoria were hung in colonial offices around the world to signify royal dominion. She justified the empire using the logic that the British were merciful rulers and colonial power was a compassionate gesture, emphasizing family values and Christian ethics. One example of this is her adoption of Aina, or Sarah Forbes

Bonetta as she was renamed.[13] Aina was a princess of the Egabo clan who had been taken prisoner by the King of Dahomey. British officers negotiated her 'freedom' and 'gifted' her to Victoria in 1850, after which she was shipped to England, renamed and treated as Victoria's godchild. Victoria also initiated what we would now call state visits – royal ceremonial tours of colonies to cement relationships between sovereign and colonial subjects,[14] a model that continues today.

Royals' approval and funding of colonial voyages and the slave trade had material benefit. Victoria openly wore the Koh-i-Noor diamond – one of the world's largest – in her crown after it was looted from the Sikh Empire in 1842, and it remains part of the Crown Jewels despite intense debate about its ownership today.[15] In 2020, the then chief curator of Historic Royal Palaces, Lucy Worsley, announced that they would be commissioning studies into histories of slavery and colonialism in royal properties. Worsley said that the properties used by the Stuart dynasty in the 17th century – including Kensington Palace and Hampton Court Palace – would 'have an element of money derived from slavery'.[16] At the time of writing, these studies are ongoing. Elsewhere, historian Brooke Newman discovered a document from 1689 showing that King William III, who built Kensington Palace, profited from shares in the Royal African Company that were gifted to him by slave trader Edward Colston.[17] Given that studies have found that a third of the 300 properties cared for by the National Trust have multiple connections to the British empire, it seems reasonable to assume many more connections will be found between royal properties and empire as these studies progress.[18]

## 'Our great imperial family to which we all belong'

Elizabeth II was crowned in 1953 with much of the British empire intact; by the end of her reign it was extinct. She avoided questions of colonial crimes, and instead positioned herself as the head of a 'voluntary' community that 'promotes democracy': the Commonwealth. This is despite the fact that some of the bloodiest consequences of empire occurred during her time as monarch, such as the Mau Mau rebellion where between 1952 and 1963, 90,000 Kenyans were executed, tortured or injured during a war between the Kenya Land and Freedom Army (the Mau Mau) and the British authorities; and apartheid in South Africa, largely intensified by the racial segregation that empire instituted.[19]

The Commonwealth itself raises questions about coloniality. On its website, it describes itself as 'a voluntary association of 56 independent and equal countries', and although it admits its 'roots go back to the British Empire', it immediately offsets that by claiming that today 'any country can join' by choice.[20] But the fact remains that the member states are former colonies (many of them former colonies of the British empire) and the Commonwealth was built out of empire's dust. In 1926, prime ministers of Britain and its dominions, including Australia, Canada and South

Africa, agreed that all of the nations were equal but united by their common allegiance to the Crown, so they would come together as the British Commonwealth of Nations with the British monarchy as head of state. In 1949, the British in the *British* Commonwealth of Nations was dropped, because the nations needn't have the British monarch as head of state and could be independent. Instead, King George VI transitioned into Head of the Commonwealth, a community of independent states united by shared values.

The role of Head of the Commonwealth was passed down to Elizabeth II (see Figure 6.1) and then to Charles III, despite protests that making the role hereditary reeks of colonialism.[21] In addition, 15 of the nations remain realms, with the King as head of state. Debates rage in many of these nations about becoming independent, especially across the Caribbean. Republicanism has some public support in Australia, New Zealand and Canada, but at the time of writing it was not a political priority. Only Papua New Guinea, the Solomon Islands and Tuvalu have restated their continued support of the monarchy.[22] Unhappiness in Commonwealth realms demonstrates increasing recognition of its imperial origins.

As we saw earlier, the Commonwealth 'family' is often serviced through official state visits, where royals meet its inhabitants. Researchers have pointed out that the presentation of the royals as celebrities during these visits obscures histories of colonialism and 'maintains and displaces the white diasporic ties between Commonwealth ... nations'.[23] In the

**Figure 6.1: Queen Elizabeth II visiting New Zealand**

Newly crowned Queen Elizabeth II, accompanied by Prince Philip, visiting Auckland Hospital in New Zealand as part of her six-month Commonwealth tour, 24 December 1953. Nurses from the hospital line the street to greet the royals.

celebration of royalty, indigenous or local communities play a supporting role as background characters, there only to celebrate the presence of overseas royals who are deified and positioned as superior. For example, media stories describing royals as meeting 'tribe members' homogenize indigenous communities in hierarchical terms, with their individual identity or even their tribe identity apparently irrelevant.[24] Vague notions of 'tribes' or 'Aboriginal communities' are used to illustrate the monarchy's apparent inclusivity, rather than representing indigenous communities themselves. They exist *in relation to* the royal that they meet. Likewise, the notion of a global 'family' conceals the power relations inherent to settler coloniality and royalty, where, by very virtue of their positions, they are not equal.

The optics of state visits are often problematic. In 2012, William and Kate visited the Solomon Islands and were carried on throne-like chairs by locals.[25] Charles and Camilla were widely criticized for laughing during an Inuit throat-singing performance in Iqaluit, Nunavut, in 2017.[26] The latter positions the local communities as what social scientists would refer to as 'other' – different from the white, Western royals, and implicitly inferior.[27] This coloniality ensures Western dominance, as indigenous communities become spectacle for entertainment.

### Coloniality and the monarchy

Given the complex history of monarchy and empire, it is not surprising that evocations of colonialism are the driving force behind many countries' fights for independence (see Box 6.1). For example, Marlene Malahoo Forte, Jamaica's minister for legal and constitutional affairs, said that becoming a republic would be 'saying goodbye to a form of government that is linked to a painful past of colonialism and the transatlantic slave trade'.[28] These systems of global violence and extraction of resources from colonized lands and peoples are powerful arguments for abolishing the monarchy, and for wider reckonings

## Box 6.1: Victoria toppled

Queen Victoria's rule over 'the empire on which the sun never sets' is commemorated in the huge range of things that bear her name across the globe. The name 'Victoria' variously refers to: a state in Australia, a provincial capital in Canada, a capital city in the Seychelles, a harbour in Hong Kong, a lake in Uganda, a waterfall in Zimbabwe, a shopping zone in South Africa, a memorial in India, a park in New Zealand, and a mountain in Belize.[29] This is in addition to the hundreds of portraits and statues of Victoria and other British royals around the world.

These objects and areas have been the focus of many anti-racist and decolonization protests. In 2024, a bronze statue of Victoria was toppled by activists in Geelong, Victoria, who spray-painted 'the colony can fall' on the stone plinth. Another statue of her in Melbourne was vandalized with red paint.[30]

Following the Black Lives Matter movement and widening global consciousness around racial inequalities, toppling monuments to slavery and other problematic histories has increasingly become an activist tactic. Revolutionary anti-racist theorist Frantz Fanon wrote that colonialism is 'a world of statues'.[31] These statues memorialize inequality, in that they often reference war, conquest, whiteness and sovereign rule. They reveal to us a hierarchy of belonging in public space, of what or who should be commemorated, and what or who should be forgotten. In toppling statues, protesters make the case that statues and other symbols are not banal, but normalize and celebrate structures of inequality. Victoria's eponyms should not be dismissed as quirks of history – they are as important in reproducing a colonial imagination as royal visits, speeches and government systems which rely on an overseas monarch. If we want to seriously consider post-colonialism, we must also address these memorials.

with these histories and the goods and people that were stolen from local communities.

While debates about republicanism in the UK are growing, there is yet to be the consensus as in nations like Jamaica. The empire is referred to as one of the reasons why the UK *might* want to abolish the monarchy, but the empire is positioned as happening 'out there', and articulated through discourses of colonialism, with abolishing the monarchy tethered to ideas of decolonizing. Monarchism, meanwhile, is tied to ideas of what 'Britishness' (perhaps more accurately 'Englishness') is, where to abolish the monarchy would be to erase part of national identity or diminish Britain's 'global power'. This was particularly the case in the context of the Conservative government's (2010–2024) right-wing, post-imperialist, militaristic political discourse of 'Global Britain', which (re)centred monarchism in Britain's past, present and future.[32]

Such framings ignore how coloniality operates at home. Coloniality structures the composition of the welfare state,[33] migration and citizenship policies,[34] and the relative powerlessness of the UK's devolved nations, particularly Scotland and Northern Ireland.[35] The welfare state is often reduced to an issue of class inequality, migration policies reduced to issues of racialization and ethnicity, and the devolved nations as matters of party politics. But all of these are indelibly shaped by the empire, colonialism, coloniality and post-colonialism. Likewise, the notion that Britain is, or has ever been, a bounded island nation is misleading. As Gurminder Bhambra puts it, 'a *national* history is not possible' because of Britain's 'colonial entanglements'.[36] You cannot separate Britain and colonial power as though colonialism happened 'out there', because colonial power shaped what Britain is and is not.

If the language of coloniality were turned inwards, then, we might find ourselves with another way to articulate the discomfort of monarchical rule. Monarchy did not just fund and enable colonial voyages and the transatlantic slave trade as it happened *out there* – a Eurocentric framing of active colonizers and passive colonized peoples. Rather, monarchy's investment in the slave trade shaped the coloniality upon which contemporary Britain is built and continues to rely. The death of Elizabeth II has prompted many global realms to feel ready to embrace independence, and likewise it should also trigger a reckoning with how coloniality operates at home, and how the people of Britain (whatever their citizenship or migration status) could reclaim democracy and equality. White settler nations like Australia might offer a way into this. Unlike colonialism, where the goal is to maintain inequalities between the colonizer and the colonized to ensure systems of superiority/inferiority, in settler colonialism the colonized and the colonizer occupy the same territory, and processes of dispossession and displacement aim to create, in Australia for instance, a white majority state. If we assume forms of racism are at play in how Britain imagines its former colonies (which they are), abolishing the monarchy in a white settler nation like Australia perhaps makes it more imaginable to Britons than it does in other former colonies, whose cultures and norms are 'othered' and seen as 'further' from a white, British norm. This is partly speculation of course, but it is interesting to consider how coloniality and republicanism intersect, with the caveat that republican France shows us that disentanglement from and a reckoning with colonial legacies is not only a task for monarchies. By teasing out the connections between republicanism and the language of coloniality, we can reconfigure how monarchy's 'colonial entanglements' are understood.

# 7

# CUSTODIANS
# OF THE LAND?

Myth: 'Fretting over "land inequality" is a waste of time.'
Ross Clark, journalist, 2019[1]

When William the Conqueror invaded England in 1066 and was crowned king, he declared that all land belonged to the Crown. He then parcelled out portions of it to his most loyal nobles, barons and the church, to keep them as allies.[2] These allies then distributed some of *their* land to various other tenants lower down in the social structure. This process is known as feudal tenure. Aside from the monarch, none of these people actually *owned* the land they were portioning out. They were just leasing it from somebody else (*leasehold*), and usually had to pay for it in some way. This could be feudal dues, taxes or rents to those higher up the social structure, or through labour or military service. Eventually, this developed into land also being given to people paying a one-off, monetary fee (*freehold*). Ultimately, as the landowner, it was the monarch who benefited from this system.

What many people do not realize is that the Crown is *still* the owner of everything. All land in England and Wales is ultimately owned by the Crown, and freehold and leasehold titles are 'held of the Crown'.[3] Of course, as King Charles is not immediately seeking to seize control of your garden, this is often dismissed as a quirk of history. But in fact, if you die without a will and no traceable relatives can be found, any land you own will return to the Crown thanks to the law of *bona vacantia*. And even if we consider this as merely symbolic, the symbolism of one institution being the ultimate owner of all land embeds deep inequalities, where all citizens are subjects to a powerful entity.

Landownership is a deeply complex topic in Britain, a country where land and power are perhaps more tightly intertwined than anywhere else. Before the House of Lords Act 1999 abolished hereditary peers inheriting a seat in the House of Lords, many of the top landowners sat at the centre of political power.[4] Today, more than half of England is owned by less than 1 per cent of the population, typically corporations and members of the aristocracy.[5] All of this comes from the monarchy's introduction of feudalism, and the ongoing protection of hereditary power, which means that wealth has remained within a select few families for the last thousand years.[6] The previous Duke of Westminster (1951–2016), who was worth £8.6 billion because of his family's property portfolio that includes 300 acres of central London, was asked to give advice to entrepreneurs aspiring to be as rich as he was. He replied, 'make sure they have an ancestor who was a very close friend of William the Conqueror'.[7] This shows how ancient rites still hold power nearly a millennium later. As we will see, despite Clark claiming it's a waste of time to be concerned, both monarchy and the aristocracy have benefited from these systems of inequality.

## What land does the monarchy own, and why?

Regent Street is one of London's best-known sites: 1.3 kilometres long, it is lined with famous shops, bars and restaurants, including Hamleys, the world-famous toy shop. This is about as prime as real estate gets, at the heart of one of the world's most expensive cities. What you might not know about Regent Street is that it is almost entirely owned by one company: the Crown Estate.

The Crown Estate is one of Europe's largest real estate empires, with a value of £15.8 billion in 2023.[8] It also owns half of St James's Street in London (another historic space), retail and leisure parks across the UK, hundreds of thousands of hectares of agricultural land and forests, and most of the UK's seabed and coastline.[9] It belongs to the reigning monarch 'in right of the Crown'.[10] That means that it is not the private property of the monarch (so they cannot sell it), but it is owned by a monarch for the duration of their reign, and then passed to their successor. The Crown

Estate's website will tell you that 'our purpose is to create lasting and shared prosperity for the nation'.[11] Much like the monarchy itself, the estate is positioned through a kind of soft power, as a trustee representing and advocating for the people's interests. Yet, there are very real material and economic benefits to the estate. The estate is run as a commercial business, with capital profit being the key driver. The annual revenue from the estate is given to the Treasury, ostensibly in exchange for the Sovereign Grant: the money that funds all of monarchy's 'official' business. Critics of the estate have pointed out that were its assets nationalized, this would contribute much more to public life.[12]

The Crown Estate is just one tiny part of the monarchy's extraordinary wealth. The primary land and property holdings of the monarchy are shown in Table 7.1. Landownership in the UK is notoriously difficult to calculate, as 17 per cent of land remains unregistered with the Land Registry, but this list alone amounts to 865,000 acres of land.[13]

All of the monarchy's landownership benefits from archaic laws of royal privilege, and the monarchy remains an anomaly. Royal wills are kept sealed, meaning that we cannot know the precise status of those estates owned personally by members of the royal family.[14] As aforementioned, the Crown Estate revenue is surrendered to the government in return for government funding, to give the impression that the amount of funding they receive via the Sovereign Grant is tied to how well the Crown Estate has performed

**Table 7.1: The monarchy's primary land and property holdings**

| Type/ name | Status of landownership | Approximate assets |
|---|---|---|
| Privately owned property[15] | The same way as other citizens own land and property | Includes: Sandringham Estate, 20,000 acres; Balmoral Estate, 50,000 acres; and the nearby Delnadamph Estate, 7,000 acres |
| The Crown Estate[16] | The reigning monarch 'in right of the Crown' | A Freedom of Information request revealed that the Estate does not have a record of its precise holdings, but estimate it to be about 615,000 acres; this includes Regent's Park (see Figure 7.1), half of St James's Street, retail and leisure parks, 115,000 hectares of agricultural land and forests, and 55 per cent of UK foreshore |
| The Duchy of Cornwall[17] | Owned by the heir to the throne in their role as the Duke of Cornwall, from a Royal Great Charter in 1337 | 135,000 acres of land and 5,000 acres of foreshore; this includes 18,710 acres of land in Cornwall, half of the Dartmoor Estate, the majority of the Isles of Scilly, some holdings in Herefordshire and Somerset, and Poundbury in Dorset |
| The Duchy of Lancaster[18] | Owned by the sovereign as Duke of Lancaster, classified as 'an inalienable asset of the Crown, held in trust for future sovereigns' | 45,550 acres, including the Savoy Estate in London, Lancaster Castle, rural estates including Crewe Hall, Myerscough, Wyreside, Whitewell, and the Lancashire foreshore (from the River Mersey to Barrow in Furness) |

that year, even though this is essentially a fabrication.[19] The Duchy of Cornwall is not registered as a company, so it does not pay corporation tax, but nor is it a charity or a public body (despite the fact it is accountable to the Treasury and to parliament). The Duchy's annual

**Figure 7.1: Monogrammed bollards in Regent's Park, London**

Bollards monogrammed with the royal cypher for Queen Elizabeth II, in the Outer Circle of Regent's Park, London, 26 November 2007. Regent's Park is part of the Crown Estate.

reports describe it as a 'private estate', which means it is not subject to Freedom of Information law.[20] And it benefits from the unique privileges of Crown exemption, leaving it not legally liable for capital gains tax, inheritance tax or income tax.[21]

All of this means that there is little transparency about how the estates are run or how the money is spent. There have been a few debates about whether the Duchies and their income belong to the monarchy or the public.[22] In 1649 after the English Civil War, Oliver Cromwell seized the Duchies for the state, but upon the restoration of monarchy they returned to Charles II. In the 1830s and the 1900s, the House of Commons debated whether Duchy revenues should go to the public purse (this was ultimately rejected). In 2005, the House of Commons Committee of Public Accounts published a report which recommended that the Duchies' accounts must become 'clearer and more transparent', the role of various royals and bodies (like the Treasury) needed to be made clearer to avoid conflicts of interest, and:

> There should be an assessment of how well the surpluses of the two Duchies correspond to the respective needs of the Households of the Queen and the Prince of Wales. The current arrangements stem from the fourteenth century, and the resulting income is to that extent an accident of history.[23]

The report's recommendations for a large-scale review have been ignored by the government, but the arguments demonstrate how many aspects of the Duchies have not changed for centuries, despite the socio-political context within which the Duchies operate changing beyond recognition.

While in some ways the estates have remained the same, they have also benefited hugely from the surge in land and property prices we have seen over the last few decades. In 2000, the Duchy of Lancaster income was just over £10 million. In 2022, it was over £28 million.[24] Landed wealth is often dismissed as archaic and obsolete, but in fact as those figures show, it is still a powerful force of capital accumulation. In late capitalism, this has been called the 'rentier' economy[25] or the 'asset economy',[26] whereby property and asset ownership are increasingly determining class position once more. Indeed, 'new money' (for example, global conglomerate business owners, tech moguls, self-made billionaires) owns 17 per cent of English land,

and companies and limited liability partnerships own 18 per cent.[27] Land is a very valuable commodity.

There are also changes in how the estates are using the land. *The Guardian*'s report on the Duchies refers to their 'long-term investment strategy', moving away from a portfolio that was predominantly rural farmland, and is now increasingly more profitable urban land.[28] For the Duchy of Lancaster this includes a business centre in Essex and an industrial estate in Salford, and for the Duchy of Cornwall, the Oval cricket ground in south London and a Crowne Plaza hotel in Reading. These are strategic investments made to secure the estate's future in a changing world, where building, selling and/or renting private and commercial property is hugely profitable, while aristocrats sitting in their massive, crumbling mansions are no longer economically viable. Many have had to give their estates, or at least part of them, to organizations like the National Trust, which can afford to maintain historical spaces through charitable donations and tourist income. Other estate owners have done this themselves. The Earl of Devon recently referred to his inherited estate, Powderham Castle, as 'an 800-year-old start-up', reflecting how many owners have developed their country houses as small and large businesses, with teams of professional staff (marketing, PR), commercial ventures (weddings, holiday cottages, zoos) and social media influencing.[29] This brings together the feudal and the capitalist (see Box 7.1), as archaic estates are commercialized under the asset boom of late capitalism.

## Box 7.1: Feudal injustice

'Totally feudal and unjust', is how one resident described the Duchy of Cornwall's presence in the Isles of Scilly.[30]

The Duchy owns most of the land and almost one-third of the residential buildings on the islands, giving its tenants leaseholder status of their properties. In the rest of the UK, leaseholders have a legal right to buy the freehold of their property if they meet a set of qualifying criteria, but an exemption has been applied to Duchy property. This means that no residents can become freeholders, they struggle to sell their homes because the leasehold is too short, and they cannot borrow against their properties for things like care fees. It also means that tenants have to pay the Duchy an annual rent.

Residents have long asked why the Duchy has been granted exemption. One resident submitted a Freedom of Information request to discover if Charles had lobbied government ministers to get the exemption, but the government rejected the request. The Guardian has since discovered, as part of its scrutiny of the Queen's consent that we saw in Chapter 2, that Charles was allowed to approve the contents of three acts relating to the exemption, including the Leasehold Reform Act 1967, although they did not unearth any proof that he lobbied the government for changes.[31]

The Duchy claims it does not sell freehold land to 'protect and preserve these buildings and their surrounding natural environment for future generations', positioning itself as a custodian of the land.[32] This is even though classification schemes like 'listed buildings' exist in the Isles of Scilly, just like they do everywhere else in the UK. The Duchy actively ignores multiple complaints from residents that it is undemocratic, unjust and removes their legal rights, and it is permitted to operate differently from other landowners because of its royal connections.

## Relationships with the aristocracy

As we saw earlier, historically, alignments between the monarchy and the aristocracy or landed gentry were materially visible. Many aristocrats received gifts of land, peerages and pensions from the monarch, during wartime the default position was that the peerage would support the king in battle, and the royal court, where both royals and aristocrats were to be found, was the hub of national, political power.[33] Over time, aristocracy's presence in the social and political landscape has become less visible. For example, after the Reform Act 1832, voting in elections was no longer reserved for men who owned land.

But this does not mean that the aristocracy is in decline, despite what some sociologists have claimed,[34] and we saw how they have increasingly diversified their portfolios to try and retain wealth. They continue to adorn the pages of specialist magazines like *Tatler* as part of high society. The close relationship between monarchy and aristocracy endures, with many historical 'quirks' still intact. Until the wedding of William and Kate, the vast majority of royal marriages were within the aristocratic classes, further cementing their mutual interests. Partners were chosen strategically for diplomatic, financial or dynastic alliance. Ladies-in-waiting are personal assistants to royal women, and are always the preserve of aristocrats as a form of unpaid service.[35] 'Traditional' activities like hunting or polo are dominated by the upper classes and nurture mutually beneficial relationships. Elite schools are one area extensively studied by sociologists, as places that perpetuate the status of privileged groups through gatekeeping access.[36] The Queen had 30 godchildren, of whom at least 14 were aristocrats or landed gentry, King Charles has 33 godchildren with at least 13 being aristocrats or landed gentry, Prince William has six godparents, of whom at least four are aristocrats or landed gentry. These are close relationships that are actively nurtured and preserved over time.

Sociologist Pierre Bourdieu would refer to these activities as acts of accumulating 'cultural capital' or inculcating a value system. That is, they socialize the royals and the aristocracy in the manners, values, tastes, styles and vocabulary of the upper classes.[37] Cultural capital is a primary form of exclusivity, ensuring anyone who does not embody appropriate capital is not valued in elite circles. This upholds a system of class domination, in which *belonging* to a particular group is understood as the most important factor in the designation of social class.

It also means that the social relationships between aristocracy and monarchy remain, and they have mutual interests in upholding one another. We saw in Chapter 2 that the monarchy retains lobbying power beyond anything most people can imagine, and that the royals have lobbied on things like land laws. These also benefit a landowning aristocracy. In a highly stratified class system, there is much to be said for 'who you know', and having the ear of the King to whisper in is potentially beneficial.

It is not really surprising that the monarchy and the aristocracy might have close relationships, given their historical connections. But we have seen in other chapters how the royals trade on performances of 'ordinariness' (they 'work', they partner with charities) or symbolism (they represent the nation, they are celebrities), both of which detract from material systems of capital accumulation, elitism and hereditary power. There are also stereotypes of the aristocracy as out-of-touch, eccentric and decadent, which the royals have partly avoided (although Charles has long been described as unconventional). This means that the royals have partly been able to distance themselves from the debauchery of the aristocratic classes and instead align themselves with 'the people'. This is hugely ideologically powerful. While the aristocracy are laughed at, the royals exist in a space beyond them, while simultaneously reaping all the rewards that come with being part of a privileged class. Additionally, and somewhat contradictorily, the presence of the monarchy upholds the aristocratic system. Monarchy's association with national identity and national history benefits the aristocracy, as their country estates are similarly associated with vague notions of Britishness (or, Englishness). Tourism on these estates is partly tourism of a quaint, rural, opulent version of the nation. Without one another, the monarchy and the aristocracy would be in trouble, both materially and ideologically.

## Landed power

If we really want to understand what the monarchy is for, we need to explore how it acquired and maintains its wealth and class privilege. While there are other avenues through which the monarchy accumulates wealth – such as collections of artwork and jewellery – landed wealth speaks to a particular history of Britain. British land has been indelibly shaped by the monarchy and the aristocratic classes, both in its design (the rolling fields marked by hedgerow boundaries, which were cultivated by aristocratic landowners to delineate ownership) and in the politics of its ownership (land given by the monarch to their allies as part of feudal tenure, and then inherited across generations). The remarkable difficulty of accounting for landownership in the UK shows us that it is only by exposing the details that we can begin to make sense of landed power.

# 8
# TWENTY-FIRST CENTURY
# FEMINISTS?

Myth: '[The Queen was] the ultimate feminist. She's
the breadwinner. She's the one on our coins and
banknotes. Prince Philip has to walk behind her ... she's
no shrinking violet.'

Olivia Colman, actor, who played the Queen
in Netflix series *The Crown*, 2019[1]

In arguments such as the one made by Colman that
the Queen was feminist, power, visibility and social
justice are being confused. Of course, having women
(or any marginalized communities) in positions of
(hyper)visible power is valuable, because it means
those communities are represented. The more people
are represented, the more others of similar identities
feel that a position of power is available to them,
too. But as decades of critical feminist scholarship
will tell us, feminism is not simply about being a

visible woman in public life, and visibility does not necessarily equal progress. Feminism seeks social justice beyond just equality between two binary sexes (male and female); it is also about gender, sexuality, race, ethnicity, disability, body type, nationality and class. That is, feminism is a project that seeks to dismantle intersectional inequalities. Like other famous women in British political life, Margaret Thatcher and Theresa May, the Queen was not automatically feminist because of her gender, and the monarchy is not somehow progressive or modernized because it includes a history of powerful women. The simplest way we can debunk that argument is that the rule of male-preference primogeniture, which dictated that males would always be crowned in preference to females, was only lifted in 2011. Powerful so-called 'feminist' queens, then – from Elizabeth I and Victoria to Elizabeth II – were only crowned because there was no male heir to take their place. We should not base our argument about whether the Queen and the monarchy are feminist on the individual characteristics or intentions of a few, but rather on the characteristics of the institution. And, as we will discuss in this chapter, the monarchy is patriarchal to its core.

## From the 'virgin queen' to the 'people's princess'

Let's first consider the gendered and racialized ways that women in the monarchy have been represented. Elizabeth I came to the throne in 1558 amidst extreme socio-political upheaval and change, after the violent

rule of her father Henry VIII, short reigns of her
siblings Edward VI and Mary I, and the Reformation
(the religious revolution which led to the creation
of Protestantism) and the Counter-Reformation (the
Catholic resurgence). Technological development had
led to increased global trade opportunities, military
threat, colonization and expansion. This gave rise
to multiple wars, the formation of the East India
Company to trade in the Indian Ocean region, and
initial attempts to colonize the Americas. Elizabeth I
never married, so was famously considered the 'virgin
queen', and this was used in highly gendered ways
to symbolize England's supposed virtue. England's
defeat of the Spanish Armada in 1588, for example,
was understood in public culture as symbolic of God's
favour and England's purity (see Figure 8.1).[2] This was
associated with the piety attached to women's sexual
morality, and women's bodies being understood as
representative of the nation. We can see other cases
where queen and country are conflated. Elizabeth I
often spoke of being married to her kingdom, referring
to 'all my husbands, my good people' in 1599.[3] One
of her most famous lines, 'I know I have the bodie,
but of a weak and feeble woman, but I have the heart
and Stomach of a King, and a King of England too',
contrasts her 'feeble' feminine natural body with her
'innate' masculine strength, passed down through a
genealogical lineage of powerful male kings.[4] Said in
the context of the impending invasion of the Spanish
Armada, this metaphor is used to describe the country
itself, as the Armada are warned that Elizabeth/the

**Figure 8.1: 'The Armada Portrait' of Elizabeth I by George Gower, c. 1588**

The portrait signified England's military strength and was made to commemorate the defeat of the Spanish Armada, depicted in the background.

country may appear weak, but Her/its body politic are as strong as ever.

These representations of Elizabeth I are also heavily racialized. In her application of makeup and in the design of her portraits, her white skin was emphasized by painting it lighter. Such visions of a 'pure', white, 'virgin' queen reify white power, particularly in the context of increasing cosmopolitanism and multiracial communities in England, colonizing the Americas and their native populations, and keeping hold of England's control of Ireland, where its native population were considered 'less white' (and therefore less privileged) than the English.[5] Nearly 300 years later, Queen Victoria similarly represented an idealized racial image, with pale skin, white hair and pearl necklaces. Her portrait hung in colonial offices across the British empire, to 'make white rule of the non-white seem normative'.[6] The queens' images symbolize white supremacy and colonial domination.

Femininity also plays an important role in mediating queens, and Victoria's gender repositioned the British monarchy under shifting relations of social and political power. Victorian industrialization established the middle classes as a class, sitting between the aristocratic upper classes and the poorer working classes, who had traditionally been either side of a feudalist binary. The middle classes were characterized by the separate spheres of work and home, where middle-class respectability (and hence moral superiority from the classes either side of them) was symbolized by a nuclear, heteronormative family, presided over by the husband/father and cared for by the wife/mother, who stayed at home. Victoria embodied this family morality. While previously the royal court had been represented as the centre of national political power, Victoria's reign featured portraits of interior domestic scenes and 'family life', with her as dutiful wife and mother. This was, of course, despite the army of governesses working in the background, or indeed the wealth and power of the royals, which meant they were definitely not middle class. Middle-class wives typically acted as public symbols of their husbands' values and status, and Victoria's embracing of this ideology allowed her to act as a symbol of the nation's value and status.[7] We could still see this during Elizabeth II's reign, with the Queen depicted as the nation's 'elderly grandmother'. 'Soft power' is centralized as a vehicle for monarchism.

On a different note, Princess Diana's embodiment of white femininity speaks to the post-colonial, post-imperial, neoliberal conjuncture that characterized the final two decades of the 20th century. Her performance of white motherhood, consumption of Western fashion culture and global humanitarianism have all been analysed as 'script[s] of white femininity'.[8] The many photographs of her hugging Black children in Africa, for example, can be read as representative of the 'white saviour' logic we see in global charity work, or in the white celebrities who adopt children of colour to 'rescue' them (à la Madonna or Angelina Jolie).[9] Diana was popularly termed 'the people's princess' because she was seen to refuse the elitism of the rest of the royal family and instead was in touch with 'ordinary people'. But this assumes that 'the people' see themselves represented in a white, upper-class, heterosexual, cis-gender woman, or at least that her privileged identity doesn't matter for her representative value in transnational contexts. Such assumptions centralize whiteness as the norm, reproduced through repetition in myths, images and discourses of an idealized princess figure.

Many critical race theorists have described whiteness as 'invisible'.[10] That is, we do not see it because we take it for granted as the norm, against which all else is defined. It is only when its status is disrupted that we recognize its power. Arguably, this was the case when Meghan Markle joined the royal family in 2018. At first, her marriage to Prince Harry was celebrated as a 'modernization' of the monarchy, demonstrative of how the monarchy and the UK were 'post-racial' because they had embraced the diversity of contemporary Britain.[11] But within a few short months, Markle was repeatedly positioned by the British press (and to a lesser extent international media) as an 'outsider' to the institution. This spanned from a BBC presenter tweeting a racist image of Harry and Meghan holding hands with a chimpanzee wearing clothes, captioned 'royal baby leaves hospital', to tabloid reports of Markle being 'difficult' or 'strong-willed', which draw on the racist and sexist stereotype of the 'angry Black woman'.[12] Repeatedly, Markle was compared with the rest of the royals, who were seen to 'belong' to the institution because they 'behave appropriately', which also has sexist and racist undertones. As we now know, the onslaught from the UK tabloid media, and their treatment by the royal family itself, led to Harry and Meghan leaving the monarchy and estranged them from the rest of the royals. The most powerful symbol of monarchical progress of the 21st century, a mixed-race princess, was forced out.

Critical race scholar Kehinde Andrews argues that 'hailing a Black royal as a sign of supposedly "modern" Britain is in fact symbolic violence, part of a discourse designed to legitimise continued racial oppression by masking it'.[13] Likewise, the normalization of whiteness in the monarchy masks the ideological function of white supremacy. As we saw in Chapter 6, monarchy is a vehicle of imperial nostalgia that, with it, legitimizes systems of white power.

## Divorced, beheaded, died; divorced, beheaded, survived

Many of us will be familiar with this rhyme, taught in UK schools as a tool to remember the fate of Henry VIII's wives. Henry VIII was (in)famous for taking six wives in his pursuit of a male heir, and punished women for failing to provide him with one. His first marriage to Catherine of Aragon was annulled (not divorced, despite what the rhyme says) and she was sent away, never seeing her daughter Mary (later Mary I) again; and both Anne Boleyn and Catherine Howard were accused of adultery and beheaded so Henry could marry other women. The light-heartedness of the rhyme belies the underlying story of violence against women, misogynistic power over women's bodies and reproductive capacities, and primogeniture in favour of sons (two of Henry's wives gave birth to daughters who were not considered worthy of becoming heir apparent, although, ironically, both eventually did succeed to the throne as Mary I and Elizabeth I). The story reminds us that without women's reproductive capacities, the monarchy as an institution cannot itself be reproduced. Royal women's bodies are an intensely political project. As Hilary Mantel famously wrote, 'a royal lady is a royal vagina'.[14]

Political and public obsession with royal women's wombs has a long history. After the restoration of monarchy in 1660 and amidst increasing tensions between Catholics and Protestants, the Duke of York – widely feared a practising Catholic – tried to produce an heir before his crowning as James II in 1685. His failure to do so prompted a dynastic crisis. In 1688, his wife Mary of Modena gave birth to a baby boy, who would be raised Catholic. In response, James' enemies spread a rumour that James and Mary's baby had been stillborn, and another live baby had been smuggled into Mary's bedroom in a warming pan to be presented as the male heir. William of Orange took advantage of the doubts about the legitimacy of the birth to justify his invasion, and later disposed of James II to become king.[15] After this incident, it became custom that the Home Secretary should be present at all royal births: a tradition which only ended in 1948 with the birth of Prince Charles. Elsewhere, after Princess Diana and Kate Middleton wed their respective princes, the media obsessively speculated on their fertility and potential pregnancies in search of a legitimate heir.[16] This is not just about the birth of a baby, rather (white) royal women's bodies are used 'as a biological and social reproducer of the nation's future'.[17] To birth a prince is to birth the future of the country (see Box 8.1).

The silly rhyme about Henry VIII's wives highlights the relationship between British history and misogyny. The women become a mere footnote in familiar narratives of the 'wayward prince' or licentious king, forgiven for their violations because they add a

## Box 8.1: Hidden queer histories

The monarchy relies on heterosexuality for its continuation. The structure of succession as set out in the Act of Settlement 1701, whereby one inherits if they are a direct descendant of the throne, means 'legitimate' births are tied to heterosexual relationships.

Accusations of queerness were historically used to discredit royals, because they had the potential to damage their claims to the throne as they called into question 'legitimate' succession. Of course, public understandings of gender and sexuality have shifted drastically over time, but historians have speculated on hidden queer histories of the monarchy.[18] Edward II was rumoured to have a male lover, his political ally Piers Gaveston. James VI and I is said to have had a relationship with George Villiers, 1st Duke of Buckingham. In the painting 'Apollo and Diana' by Gerrit Van Honthorst (1628), the two men are seen ignoring their spouses and gazing intently at one another. Queen Anne was said to have had relationships with two women, her Mistress of the Robes Sarah Churchill and Sarah's cousin Abigail Masham. Elizabeth I is probably the most well-known royal rumoured to be gay, but there is no historical evidence for this, and we could attribute this to the problematic assumption that any woman who chooses not to enter a heterosexual marriage is queer.

In more recent years, Lord Ivar Mountbatten was the first member of the monarch's extended family to have a same-sex wedding, when he married his partner James Coyle in 2018.[19]

It is worth considering what impact a more prominent royal coming out as queer might have today. The accounts we see of royals who were never able to publicly embrace their sexualities (if they wanted to) are partly a sign of the times, in that queerness was poorly understood and heavily stigmatized, if not even criminalized. Today, most queer lives are more widely accepted in the UK. But the laws about royal succession remain, and while the Succession to the Crown Act 2013 abolished male-preference primogeniture, there have been no moves to allow adopted children, for example, to inherit the throne. The monarchy is also, as we have seen in this chapter, extremely conservative in its presentation of gender and sexuality. Can we imagine a scenario where queerness could exist in the monarchy?

little flair to British history.[20] It has been common in monarchical history for royals to marry strategically (for example, to foster alliances with powerful inter/national families) and then have extramarital relations. Henry I is said to have had around 20 illegitimate children, and Edward VII is thought to have had more than 50 affairs.[21] Prince Charles' affair with Camilla Parker Bowles made headlines around the world when Diana spoke about it on her infamous *Panorama* interview, and was it recently dramatized in *The Crown*. Such behaviour is expected from kings, contrasted with the sexual purity of queens.

In more recent years, the best-known story of sexual impropriety comes from Prince Andrew, his friendship with convicted sex offender Jeffrey

Epstein, and accusations against Andrew himself of sexual assault of a trafficked minor. Virginia Giuffre filed a civil lawsuit against him for allegedly sexually assaulting her when she was 17, and it was settled out of court in February 2022. His response to the accusations demonstrates the exceptionality permitted to royal princes. In November 2019, he voluntarily took part in an interview for BBC *Newsnight* with journalist Emily Maitlis, apparently with the aim of rescuing his public profile (the decisions leading to the interview were subsequently dramatized in Netflix film, *Scoop*).[22] But instead of exonerating himself, Andrew exposed the patriarchal privilege at the heart of monarchy. He showed no remorse towards Epstein's trafficking victims, gave increasingly far-fetched reasons why the accusations against him were false (including claiming he did not meet Giuffre the night she said because he was in a Pizza Express restaurant in Woking), and said he did not regret his friendship with Epstein because 'the people that I met and the opportunities that I was given to learn either by him or because of him were actually very useful'. This prioritizes his networking opportunities over the victims of sexual assault.

Andrew's behaviour, both alleged and documented, is representative of a culture of patriarchy among elite men. News about Andrew was being reported at the same time as #MeToo, a social movement documenting people's (mostly cis-women's) experiences of sexual assault, and institutionalized rape cultures. The conviction of former multi-millionaire film producer

Harvey Weinstein of rape and sexual assault in 2020, as well as other cases such as the disgraced Jimmy Savile (who was formerly King Charles' confidant and informal adviser[23]) have exposed a culture of patriarchal violence among elite men. This culture is enabled by the networks of (often powerful) people around them who keep their silence, effectively facilitating their behaviour. Prince Andrew has been removed from royal duties, had most of his patronages and titles stripped, and no longer receives public funding, but this was only after public protest at his continued privilege. The Queen used funds from the Duchy of Lancaster to pay for his legal defence,[24] and partly funded the out of court settlement that meant Andrew would be spared a trial.[25] This helped to protect the institution, as any court case against a royal has potential to be extremely damaging. In this context, it is notable that Andrew only faced consequences from the institution *after* his disastrous appearance on *Newsnight*, despite the accusations against him having existed for many years. On *Newsnight*, Andrew exposed his power and privilege: something the contemporary monarchy works hard to mask. It was this exposure that could potentially damage the institution – the accusations against Andrew could be ignored, or dismissed as him being a 'bad apple' in an otherwise progressive institution.[26] By distancing itself from Andrew, the monarchy was not seeking to dismantle patriarchal cultures, but rather protect itself against potential reputational damage or public distrust.

## Queens, not feminists

This chapter has considered how gender and race intersect in the monarchy. Claims that the monarchy is feminist because it crowns queens would seem to suggest that the monarchy is a bastion of gender equality: progressing the feminist fight by creating (symbolically) powerful women. But this is a reductive claim. As this chapter has shown, the history of gender and race in the monarchy is a history of patriarchy and white privilege, whereby cis-maleness, whiteness and heterosexuality are reproduced as the invisible norm, around which anything else is positioned as 'outside', and therefore inferior. This is not just about the characteristics or representations of individuals within the institution. It does not really matter the *intent* of Queen Victoria, Queen Elizabeth II or even Meghan Markle, and indeed we will never really know. What matters is how their presence is used to reproduce the power of a privileged institution. Monarchy reinforces a white, heterosexist norm, and maintains racial ideologies in white societies. That, too, is part of what it is for.

# PART IV
# WHAT'S NEXT?

# CONCLUSION

On 6 May 2023, the day of Charles III's coronation, I was in London joining the anti-monarchy 'Not My King' protest organized by campaign group, Republic. By the time I arrived at 10am, the meeting point in Trafalgar Square (near the Charles I statue, the king who was executed in 1649) had been sealed off by police, and a 'sub-protest' had begun gathering close to the National Gallery. The sub-protest marched through London towards Hyde Park, and at times the sea of people wearing yellow – the nominated colour of the protest – stretched as far as the eye could see down the street (see Figure 9.1). People brandished placards, and chanted 'Not my king!' and 'What do we want? Democracy!'

The size of the protest did not really make the national news. Those who did make it into Trafalgar Square were directly on the parade route and chanted as the King's procession passed. But BBC cameras were angled so that these hundreds of people were not visible on the live coronation footage. What *did* make the international news was that the chief executive officer of Republic, Graham Smith, and five other Republic team members had been arrested by police at around 7am that morning while unloading protest placards

**Figure 9.1: Republic's 'Not my king' protest at the coronation of King Charles III**

My photograph of the 'Not my king' protest in London, hosted by Republic, during the coronation of King Charles III on 6 May 2023. Pictured are protesters brandishing signs in the distinctive yellow colour of the protest, as we marched through London.

from a van.[1] They had not even started protesting. Fifty-two other people were arrested on the day.[2] Alice Chambers, a monarchist, was merely sitting close to Just Stop Oil protesters when police swarmed over to arrest the protesters before they had even started, and accidentally arrested Chambers too. She spent the entire day in custody.[3]

The heavy-handed policing of the coronation is indicative of wider anti-protest laws in the UK, where people's right to a peaceful protest has been slowly eroded under successive Conservative governments.

The Policing, Crime, Sentencing and Courts Act 2022 extended the conditions police can impose on protests, and the Public Order Act 2023 made a number of protest actions – including just carrying the materials that might aid in 'locking on' people to buildings or objects – illegal.[4] This is the explanation that was used to arrest Smith and the Republic team – the ties that were used to bind together a pack of placards were claimed to be potentially used for 'locking on'. As many critics have argued, such curtailing of the freedom to protest is a considerable abuse of human rights.[5] But the policing at monarchy events seems to also be indicative of the desire to maintain the status quo. Paul Powlesland was approached by police in Parliament Square in September 2022, during the mourning period for the Queen, while holding up a blank piece of paper, because police claimed he *might* write 'not my king' on it which *might* 'offend' people.[6] This is a wild overinterpretation by the police of the Public Order Act, which bans any signs that are abusive or threatening. Attempts to silence such small acts of dissent – *even* if Powlesland *did* write 'not my king' on the paper – is suggestive of a much broader moral panic about opposition to monarchy becoming more widespread. The same can be said of the fact that most national broadcasters did not show the extent of the protests in London on coronation day. Making visible alternative discourses around monarchy opens space for others to join in. In contrast, publicly arresting protesters is potentially quite effective in dissuading others from doing the same thing.

These tactics also seem to try to make republicanism a dirty word, connotative of criminal activity, political violence and disloyalty to the country. We often see public anti-monarchists shamed or mocked. In 2017, in the early years of my research, I naively went on BBC local radio to talk about Prince Philip's so-called 'retirement' from public duties and was promptly derided for daring to take a more critical stance by the presenter mocking every point I made. In summer 2022, during the Queen's Platinum Jubilee, a BBC 5 Live radio listener phoned in to my interview on the channel to say they were 'disgusted' that I was trying to 'ruin everyone's fun'. A much more extreme example is the treatment of former Labour leader Jeremy Corbyn, who was relentlessly disparaged for not supporting the monarchy. His refusal to sing 'God Save the Queen' during the 2015 Battle of Britain memorial service led to the *Daily Telegraph*'s headline 'Corbyn snubs Queen and country' and the *Daily Express* called it 'puerile, dogmatic, anti-British posturing'.[7] There are very few vocally anti-monarchy MPs, and the case of Jeremy Corbyn illustrates why. The right-wing press, quaking at the prospect of an openly socialist prime minister, constructed his distaste for monarchy as not *just* a distaste for monarchy but a distaste of the whole country, and hence he becomes an 'enemy of the people'. He becomes – apparently – unrepresentative, when being representative is his main role as MP. It is notable that MPs must swear allegiance to the King upon taking office. This also happens across the monarch's other global realms and is largely taken for granted. In 2022, Lidia Thorpe, an Indigenous senator for Victoria, Australia, added the word 'colonizing' into her oath, so she declared: 'I sovereign, Lidia Thorpe, do solemnly and sincerely swear that I will be faithful and I bear true allegiance to the colonizing her majesty Queen Elizabeth II.' She was chided by colleagues and made to recite the oath again.[8] But her protest drew global attention to the oath, and the coloniality it evokes.

Maintaining the status quo is very important to monarchy. While it needs to be hyper-visible so we see it and believe it, it also needs to be understood as 'normal', indivisible from everyday life. We've heard evidence of that throughout this book, for example, with assumptions around monarchy's 'inherent' connections to national identity. Monarchy does not necessarily rule because the public 'loves' it (although, of course, many do), but rather because people are largely indifferent to its existence. It is assumed as part of the status quo, and therefore irrelevant to other global concerns like rising poverty rates. Even among the left, the monarchy has long been positioned as a second-tier issue. Disrupting the status quo is vital to establishing a workable anti-monarchy movement. Lidia Thorpe did this in her addition of a single word to the oath, prompting a global conversation about colonial governance. The heavy-handed policing of the coronation also, ironically, did this. The arrests of protesters made visible the effort that goes into maintaining a monarchical state. It does not just exist in and of itself, but is rather continually produced and reproduced in the public imagination. When this is done in banal ways, we do not notice: coins with the monarch's face on, post-boxes etched with the royal cypher, royal correspondents relaying royal gossip on television news.[9] But we do take note when the form of power changes; when it becomes power*ful*. And in so doing, we expose how monarchy still exists today: a continual power that ensures it remains ever-present, yet hidden, in our imaginations. Exposing what the monarchy is for is key to achieving its abolition.

## The case for abolishing the monarchy

There are many blueprints for how we might transform monarchy for the future. Some commentators suggest that a 'slimmed down' monarchy, with curtailed powers and duties, would be best. Many reports said Charles would preside over a 'slimmed down' monarchy, because he is apparently aware that the monarchy needs to modernize.[10] This term gestures towards vague notions of 'tightening the purse strings', or making a monarchy look more palatable by reducing the number of visible members. But there is very little solid evidence of this happening. News outlets reported his coronation did so because it was shorter and smaller, but otherwise it followed much the same roadmap as the coronations of history.[11] 'Slimmed down monarchy' also seems to refer to reducing the number of royals we see on the Buckingham Palace balcony during ceremonies and the ones who get public funding. But Princess Alexandra, cousin once removed of Charles, is still counted as a working royal and lives in a grace-and-favour (free or very cheap, in return for 'services') apartment at St James's Palace, London.[12] But because we do not see her visibly 'being royal' on the balcony, she (and others) are often forgotten in accounts of royal wealth and privilege. 'Slimmed down', then, seems to mean little more than a PR exercise.

Another option sometimes bandied around is to have a 'bicycle monarchy', like the Scandinavian or Dutch monarchies. The nickname is said to come from Queen Juliana of the Netherlands' love of riding bicycles, and symbolizes a more informal approach to monarchism and ability to relate to 'the people'.[13] The Nordic monarchies are less grand than the British, with much less focus on pomp and ceremony. For example, the Dutch monarch is inaugurated, rather than coronated, and is never seen wearing a crown. This is suggested as a more palatable and democratic way of monarchy existing,[14] because it removes many of the symbols of wealth and privilege. But of course, these monarchies are still astronomically wealthy and privileged, and the existence of any sort of hereditary monarchy is inherently undemocratic.

While these would be a step in the right direction in terms of curtailing the monarchy's wealth and power, they do not go far enough in remedying the structural inequalities central to monarchical rule. Even if slimmed down meant the removal of half of its assets (which current proposals do not), the monarchy would still be extravagantly wealthy, not to mention still representative of all of the inequalities outlined in this book (patriarchy, whiteness, heteronormativity, coloniality, national identity, and so on). Slimming down the monarchy is merely scratching the surface and is unlikely to bring about meaningful social transformation. Indeed, in some ways this could make the problem worse. So much of the argument in this book is about how hidden many aspects of the monarchy are. By being less visible, a slimmed down monarchy could retain much of its power and influence while being even more immune to criticism.

So, what would more radical transformation look like? The common retort to the suggestion of abolishing the monarchy is 'we don't want a President Nigel Farage/Tony Blair/other problematic politician'. This is usually used to dismiss the conversation outright, and imagines a presidential model similar to that of the United States, where the president wields extraordinary executive power (we saw the dangers of this with President Trump). But the more likely option for the UK, and the model proposed by the campaign group Republic, is a parliamentary constitution, not hugely different to what we have now and similar to that of our closest neighbours, Ireland.[15] The existence of the Crown in its current form reduces parliament's power, giving the government power to make decisions without parliamentary agreement. Having a monarchy also means we do not have an independent, non-political head of state in a 'checks and balance' role, to ensure fairness. We saw the risks of that in Chapter 2, with the proroguing of parliament. A parliamentary constitution would mean abolishing the monarchy, formalizing a written constitution that clearly delineates the role of each part of the political system, creating an elected upper house, and electing an independent head of state. As Republic say, it would simply 'take what we have and make it democratic'.[16] This would also mean that public money spent on monarchy's upkeep could be redirected to public services (a president would be much cheaper), monarchy's lands could be returned to public ownership, and the assets they have kept from colonial pillages could be returned to their rightful owners.

What needs to happen for us to get there? Does the Interregnum in 1649–60 offer any kind of guide? This was the period when Charles I was executed after the English Civil Wars, the monarchy was abolished, and the Commonwealth of England was established as a republic. This is the only time England has not had a sitting monarch, and demonstrates the victory of Parliamentarians over Royalists. But the Commonwealth was not successful, as no stable government was established for more than a few months at a time, and little meaningful or long-term legislation was passed, which soon led to anarchy. Oliver Cromwell became Lord Protector, which was passed on to his son Richard Cromwell after Oliver's death in 1659, before their Protectorate Parliament was dissolved and the monarchy restored to Charles I's son, Charles II, in 1660. The Interregnum was also not straightforwardly an anti-monarchy movement, and historically 'republic' has not always equated to anti-monarchism, but has also been used to refer to balanced constitutions that sometimes include a monarch.[17] For many Parliamentarians, the initial aim of the English Civil Wars was not to abolish the monarchy, but to demand Parliament's participation in government. Only because Charles I refused to compromise due to his belief in the divine right of kings did he end up being tried and executed. Oliver Cromwell also *essentially* ruled just like a monarch, passing on the role to his son and being addressed as Your Highness. The Commonwealth of England hence lacked the radical vision needed to survive without the monarchy. Another downside is that the English Civil Wars were extremely bloody, with some estimates suggesting 100,000 people died.[18] Cromwell has a record of extreme brutality in Ireland, where parliament, threatened by the alliance of the Irish Confederate Catholics and the English Royalists, waged war, including massacres at Drogheda and Wexford that killed thousands of soldiers and civilians.

All of this means that the 1650s are not the place to look to make republicanism an attractive and achievable prospect. Although there have been no 'successful' (as in, they abolished the monarchy) republican movements in the UK since, others have explicitly equated republicanism with anti-monarchism. In the *Rights of Man*, philosopher Thomas Paine argued that we can never achieve equality without democracy, and his Latin phrase 'res publica', meaning 'public affair' and the root of the word 'republic', was 'naturally opposed to the word monarchy' because a monarch is not representative of the people.[19] The early 1870s saw a small-scale socialist strand of anti-monarchy republicanism concerned with class inequality. The National Republican Brotherhood, for example, took inspiration from the Paris Commune to call for the nationalization of land and the extension of welfare.[20] This never really took off, and big names like Karl Marx and Friedrich Engels didn't pay much attention to monarchy, although Marx did call it the 'indispensable cloak of class-rule'.[21] In the 1930s, the Communist Party protested the royal family 'as baleful puppets of monopoly capitalism'.[22] In 1991, democratic socialist Labour MP Tony Benn proposed the Commonwealth of Britain Bill, which would abolish the monarchy and the House of Lords, elect a president and introduce a codified constitution (see Box 9.1). It was seconded by future Labour Party leader Jeremy Corbyn, but never got a second reading in the House of Commons.[23]

These movements all demonstrate attempts to associate the monarchy with wider social issues, like class inequality, or design feasible alternatives to constitutional monarchy. Abolishing the monarchy would not have to involve war or bloodshed, nor the monarch's head on a spike. In the political satire *The Queen and I*, novelist Sue Townsend imagines the monarchy has been abolished and the Queen – now Mrs Windsor – and her family are sent to live on a council estate.[24] Of course, I am not suggesting the royals go to live on housing estates meant to improve the lives of the working classes. But they could, for example, just move to one of the many properties they already own and live out their days there. Prince Harry and Meghan Markle have shown that 'post-royal life' is possible, although of course they have done so in very different circumstances and have explicitly never stopped supporting the monarchy.

### Box 9.1: The Commonwealth of Britain Bill

Let's take a closer look at Tony Benn's Commonwealth of Britain Bill.[25]

The bill proposed that the monarchy would be abolished, the royals would become private citizens and have no exceptional legal status. They would have to work and pay taxes. The honours system would be scrapped, and the Crown Estate and the royals' other lands nationalized. The Privy Council would be disbanded, and royal prerogative powers would be transferred to parliament. The legal authority of the state would no longer reside in the monarchy.

The constitution would be formally written to codify the powers of state institutions, and it would be to this, rather than the monarch, that MPs and the Armed Forces would swear their oaths of allegiance. The bill also covered other institutions that are connected to monarchy: the House of Lords and the Church. Parliament would have two chambers that are democratically elected, the House of Commons and the House of the People, both with gender-balanced representation (it's worth pointing out here that Benn was proposing an equal male/female split, rather than accounting for all genders as we might consider today). The head of state would be a president elected by both Houses to play a ceremonial role. Scotland and Wales would have their own parliament with representatives in the House of the People, and British jurisdiction over Northern Ireland would end. The Church of England would be disestablished, and the state would exist separately from religion.

The bill was first moved in 1991 and never got a second reading, never mind the referendum that Benn proposed. The likelihood is Benn knew this would be the case, but the document serves what he called an 'educational role ... in raising aspirations', laying out what the alternative *could* look like, and why we should care. It is interesting that the bill's proposals don't just end with what we might consider to be 'the monarchy', but rather cover all manner of state and establishment organization. This demonstrates how the monarchy, or the Crown, is everywhere in British political life, and so much of what we take as commonplace stems from the existence of a monarchy.

While a Commonwealth of Britain Bill in the 2020s and beyond might look a little different, there is much we can learn from Benn's proposals and the reactions to it.

The abolishment of monarchy could play out differently around the world. Barbados became a republic in 2021, after the Barbados Labour Party acquired a more-than-two-thirds parliamentary majority and had the power to change the political system without referendum.

The model for transition followed the 1996–1998 Constitution Review Commission, with Barbados becoming a parliamentary republic and the head of state as president.[26] Other Caribbean countries such as Jamaica have announced they plan to hold referendums on abolishing the monarchy, following a similar model for reform as Barbados.

It might also look different within the UK itself. As we saw in Chapter 3, part of the argument for Scottish independence is around Scotland's subjugation to Westminster party politics and the lack of representation for Scottish politics, which are traditionally more left-wing than England's. The Scottish National Party has always said it would remain a constitutional monarchy if it became independent, but in 2023 Humza Yousaf, then-leader of the Scottish National Party, said that upon independence he would pursue a referendum on abolishing the monarchy in favour of an elected head of state.[27] A referendum on monarchy within the British Isles would have enormous impact on anti-monarchy debate. Over in Ireland, Sinn Féin are gaining popularity in the Republic due to their more left-wing policies. If Sinn Féin pursued the reunification of Ireland, the restructuring of Great Britain would foster similar debates about the British state and the constitution. The government in Westminster also affects the tenor of debate. In recent years, the Conservative Party leadership placed a renewed emphasis on the monarchy (for example, calls for the reinstatement of the royal yacht *Britannia*), post-Brexit talks debated the relevance of the Commonwealth in 'global Britain', and the royal family was used for foreign diplomacy. Although the now-sitting Labour Party have never seriously pursued anti-monarchism, and prime minister *Sir* Keir Starmer certainly does not, the change in government is likely to shift 'global Britain' and its emphasis. In many ways, how the anti-monarchy debate progresses depends on other political changes, and how society shifts alongside them. Significant political upheavals and long-term social changes are more likely to trigger change than remaining in the status quo.

We could also look within the monarchy itself. In other chapters I have outlined potential risks to popular consent for monarchy, for instance the potential political meddling of King Charles, or growing calls for the monarchy to apologize for their role in the transatlantic slave trade. If they fail to appropriately deal with these, the fallout could prompt significant anti-monarchy debate. Now the monarchy is no longer sheltered by a popular queen, it must be even more careful of how it treads. Another risk is royals 'speaking out' about their time in the monarchy. Although Prince Harry and Meghan Markle have been very clear that they are not anti-monarchists, their confessional interviews have prompted more serious critique of monarchy than anything else this century, particularly among young people, women and people of colour. While confessionals won't abolish monarchy alone, the power of personalizing the institution and exposing its inner workings should not be underestimated.

## Anti-monarchism and social justice

The title of this book asks, 'what is the monarchy for?'. My very short answer to this question is: nothing good. I have made no secret of my belief that the only way the monarchy could truly be better is if it ceases to exist. But this book has attempted to outline the complexities and multiplicities of the question. By looking at different forms of power (real, soft and hidden), we thought about the various functions of monarchy today. We broke down the 'myths' around what monarchy is *thought to be* for using alternative statistics, readings and understandings.

Monarchy has a wide range of ideological, material, political, social and cultural functions. It both upholds and relies upon a host of wider social and economic systems: whiteness, imperialism, capitalism, patriarchy, nationalism, celebrity, to name a few. To me, anti-monarchism goes hand in hand with anti-racism, feminism, decolonization, class revolution, queer liberation, disability activism and climate activism. This means that, in order to bring about radical democratic change, the abolition of monarchy is crucial, and indeed this needs to be part of a broader transition of social justice. The dawn of the new Carolean age is precisely when we should be asking, with suspicion, 'what *is* the monarchy for?'

# NOTES

## Introduction

1    Laura Clancy, '#MournHub and @GrieveWatch: Mediating monarchy and mourning in the digital age'. *International Journal of Cultural Studies*, 27(3) (2024), pp. 428–443.

2    Beth Rigby, 'David Beckham queued overnight…', X, 16 September 2022, https://twitter.com/BethRigby/status/1570796198776426496.

3    Michel Foucault, *Society Must Be Defended: Lectures at the Collège de France, 1975–1976* (Picador, 1997); Michel Foucault, *Power/Knowledge: Selected Interviews and Other Writings 1972–1977*, ed. Colin Gordon (Vintage, 1980).

## Chapter 1

1    Vernon Bogdanor and Iain McLean, 'Shifting sovereignties: Should the United Kingdom have an elected upper house and elected head of state?', *Political Insight*, 1(1) (2010), pp. 11–13.

2    Ernst Kantorowicz, *The King's Two Bodies* (Princeton University Press, 1957).

3    Seren Morris, 'Why is the Queen missing the State Opening of Parliament', *Evening Standard*, 10 May 2022, https://www.standard.co.uk/news/uk/why-queen-missing-state-opening-of-parliament-what-episodic-mobility-problems-b999079.html.

4    Vernon Bogdanor, *The Monarchy and the Constitution* (Oxford Academic, 1995), p. 1.

5    Ibid.

6    David Pegg, Rob Evans and Severin Carrell, 'King Charles to receive huge pay rise from UK taxpayers', *The Guardian*, 20 July 2023, https://www.theguardian.com/uk-news/2023/jul/20/king-charles-to-receive-huge-pay-rise-from-uk-taxpayers.

7    *Dutch News*, 'Dutch royal family budget rises 11% to €55 million', 20 September 2023, https://www.dutchnews.nl/2023/09/dutch-royal-family-budget-rises-11-to-e55-million/.

8    Rupert Neate, Henry Dyer and Ashifa Kassam, 'Windsors v Borbones: Comparing the public pay of European royal families', *The Guardian*, 5 April 2023, https://www.theguardian.com/uk-news/2023/apr/05/windsors-v-borbons-comparing-the-public-pay-of-european-royal-families#:~:text=The%20Swedish%20royal%20court%20received,%2C%20travel%2C%20staff%20and%20stables.

9    Darragh McDonagh, 'Cost of running President's office set to rise', *Irish Times*, 26 October 2021, https://www.irishexaminer.com/news/arid-40729734.html.

10    Cris Shore, 'The crown as proxy for the state?', *The Round Table*, 107(4) (2018), pp. 401–416.

11    Ibid.

12    Robert Hazell and Bob Morris (eds), *The Role of Monarchy in Modern Democracy: European Monarchies Compared* (Hart Publishing, 2020).

13    Robert Hazell and Charlotte Sayers-Carter, 'Reforming the prerogative', The Constitution Unit, 2022, https://www.ucl.ac.uk/constitution-unit/sites/constitution_unit/files/198_reforming_the_prerogative.pdf.

14    Walter Bagehot, *The English Constitution* (Chapman & Hall, 1867).

15    Peter Morgan, *The Audience* [Play] (2013–).

16    Laura Clancy and Sara De Benedictis. '"I wanted to offer my sympathy … woman to woman": Reading *The Crown* during a conjuncture of crisis', *Soundings*, 79 (2021), pp. 122–133.

17    Anne Twomey, 'From Bagehot to Brexit: The monarch's rights to be consulted, to encourage and to warn', *The Round Table*, 107(4) (2018), pp. 417–428.

18    Sir William Heseltine, 'The Queen and the constitution', *The Times*, 28 July 1986, p. 13.

19    Twomey, 'From Bagehot to Brexit'.

20    Ibid.

21    Shore, 'The crown as proxy for the state?'.

22    Norman Bonney, *Monarchy, Religion and the State* (Manchester University Press, 2013), p. 1, also includes the following quote.

23    Catherine Pepinster, *Defenders of the Faith* (Hodder & Stoughton, 2022).

24    Robert Hazell, 'Future challenges for the monarchy', Bennett Institute for Public Policy, 2022, https://www.bennettinstitute.cam.ac.uk/publications/future-challenges-for-the-monarchy/.

25    Bagehot, *The English Constitution*.

26  Stephen Brogan, *The Royal Touch in Early Modern England* (Boydell Press, 2015).

27  Ibid, p. 9.

28  Michael Ledger-Lomas, '"Daylight upon magic": Stained glass and the Victorian monarchy', *19: Interdisciplinary Studies in the Long Nineteenth Century*, 30 (2020).

29  Christianity.org, 'Queen Elizabeth II: A life of faith', 2022, https://www.christianity.org.uk/article/queen-elizabeth-ii-a-life-of-faith.

30  National Secular Society, 'Religion and the investiture of the monarch', https://www.secularism.org.uk/uploads/european-monarchy-coronation.pdf.

31  David Kim, *Religious Transformation in Modern Asia* (Brill, 2015).

32  Kōichi Mori, 'The emperor of Japan: A historical study in religious symbolism', *Japanese Journal of Religious Studies*, 6(4) (1979), pp. 522–565.

33  Shore, 'The crown as proxy for the state?'.

## Chapter 2

1  Phillip Blond, 'In defence of Kings and Queens: Why the monarch matters', BBC, 10 December 2010, https://www.bbc.co.uk/news/uk-politics-11930839.

2  Jessica Elgot and Heather Stewart, 'Boris Johnson asks Queen to suspend parliament', *The Guardian*, 28 August 2019, https://www.theguardian.com/politics/2019/aug/28/chancellor-sajid-javid-fast-tracked-spending-review-fuels-talk-of-early-election.

3  BBC News, 'Theresa May resigns over Brexit: What happened?', 24 May 2019, https://www.bbc.co.uk/news/uk-politics-48379730.

4  Kate Proctor, 'Boris Johnson's move to prorogue parliament "a constitutional outrage", says Speaker', *The Guardian*, 28 August 2019, https://www.theguardian.com/politics/2019/aug/28/boris-johnsons-move-to-prorogue-parliament-a-constitutional-outrage-says-speaker.

5  Robert Hazell and Bob Morris, *The Role of Monarchy in Modern Democracy: European Monarchies Compared* (Hart Publishing, 2020).

6  Owen Bowcott, Ben Quinn and Severin Carrell, 'Johnson's suspension of parliament unlawful, supreme court rules', *The Guardian*, 24 September 2019, https://www.theguardian.com/law/2019/sep/24/boris-johnsons-suspension-of-parliament-unlawful-supreme-court-rules-prorogue.

7   Vernon Bogdanor, *The Monarchy and the Constitution* (Oxford, 1995).

8   Republic, 'The Queen acted unlawfully, not just the PM', https://www.republic.org.uk/the_queen_acted_unlawfully_not_just_the_pm_republic.

9   David Allen Green, 'The question of whether Boris Johnson, in effect, lied to the Queen', *Law and Policy Blog*, 15 August 2022, https://davidallengreen.com/2022/08/the-question-of-whether-boris-johnson-lie-to-the-queen/.

10  House of Commons Political and Constitutional Reform Committee, 'The impact of Queen's and Prince's Consent on the legislative process', 26 March 2014, https://publications.parliament.uk/pa/cm201314/cmselect/cmpolcon/784/784.pdf.

11  Ibid, p. 9.

12  Ibid, p. 15.

13  David Pegg, Rob Evans and Michael Barton, 'Royals vetted more than 1,000 laws via Queen's consent', *The Guardian*, 8 February 2021, https://www.theguardian.com/uk-news/2021/feb/08/royals-vetted-more-than-1000-laws-via-queens-consent.

14  David Pegg and Rob Evans, 'Queen lobbied for changes to three more laws', *The Guardian*, 8 February 2021, https://www.theguardian.com/uk-news/2021/feb/08/queen-lobbied-for-changes-to-three-more-laws-documents-reveal.

15  Rob Evans, Severin Carrell and David Pegg, 'Queen secretly lobbied Scottish ministers for climate law exemption', *The Guardian*, 28 July 2021, https://www.theguardian.com/uk-news/2021/jul/28/queen-secretly-lobbied-scottish-ministers-climate-law-exemption.

16  Rob Evans, David Pegg and Severin Carrell, 'How Prince Charles pressured ministers to change law to benefit his estate', *The Guardian*, 28 June 2022, https://www.theguardian.com/uk-news/2022/jun/28/prince-charles-pressured-ministers-change-law-queen-consent.

17  Severin Carrell, Rob Evans and David Pegg, 'Queen's secret influence on laws revealed in Scottish government memo', *The Guardian*, 27 June 2022, https://www.theguardian.com/uk-news/2022/jun/27/queen-secret-influence-laws-revealed-scottish-government-memo.

18  David Pegg and Rob Evans, 'Queen lobbied for change in law to hide her private wealth', *The Guardian*, 7 February 2021,

https://www.theguardian.com/uk-news/2021/feb/07/revealed-queen-lobbied-for-change-in-law-to-hide-her-private-wealth.

19   House of Commons Political and Constitutional Reform Committee, 'The impact of Queen's and Prince's consent on the legislative process'.

20   Simon Jenkins, 'The black spider memos', *The Guardian*, 13 May 2015, https://www.theguardian.com/commentisfree/2015/may/13/black-spider-memos-prince-charles.

21   Caroline Davies, 'Charles defends political letters', *Daily Telegraph*, 26 September 2022, https://www.telegraph.co.uk/news/uknews/1408282/Charles-defends-political-letters.html.

22   Sarah Boseley, 'Did Prince Charles's letter lead Tony Blair to postpone herbal medicines law?', *The Guardian*, 13 May 2015, https://www.theguardian.com/uk-news/2015/may/13/prince-charles-letter-tony-blair-postpone-herbal-medicines-restrictions.

23   Rob Evans, 'Royal pressure "led to FoI ban on disclosure of lobbying by Charles"', *The Guardian*, 13 September 2010, https://www.theguardian.com/uk/2010/sep/13/charles-letters-freedom-information-act.

24   BBC, 'Prince Charles letters to be released after Supreme Court ruling', 26 March 2015, https://www.bbc.co.uk/news/uk-32066554.

25   Republic, *Royal Secrets*, 2015, https://assets.nationbuilder.com/republic/pages/522/attachments/original/1676474369/Republic_Royal_Secrets_Report.pdf?1676474369.

26   Ibid.

27   David Leigh, 'Secret wills of the royals: A tale of mistresses, jewels and cover-ups', *The Guardian*, 27 March 2007, https://www.theguardian.com/uk/2007/mar/27/monarchy.topstories3.

28   Laura Clancy, *Running the Family Firm* (Manchester University Press, 2021).

29   Philip Murphy, 'What the royal family can learn from MI5 about secrecy', *The Conversation*, 22 July 2015, www.theconversation.com/what-the-royalfamily-can-learn-from-mi5-about-secrecy-45023.

30   Andrew Lownie, 'The reclosure of files on the royal family: Some questions for the National Archives', *History and Policy*, 10 April 2024, https://www.historyandpolicy.org/opinion-articles/articles/the-reclosure-of-files-on-the-royal-family-some-questions-for-the-national-archives.

[31]  Index on Censorship, 'Royal secrecy surveyed', 17 January 2023, https://www.indexoncensorship.org/2023/01/royal-secrecy-surveyed/.

[32]  Laura Clancy, '"If you move in the same circles as the royals, then you'll get stories about them": Royal correspondents, cultural intermediaries and class', *Cultural Sociology*, 17(3) (2023), pp. 331–350.

[33]  Heather Brooke, *The Silent State* (Random House, 2011).

[34]  Murphy, 'What the royal family can learn from MI5 about secrecy'.

[35]  Brooke, *The Silent State*, p. 260.

[36]  Cris Shore, 'The crown as proxy for the state? Opening up the black box of constitutional monarchy', *The Round Table*, 107 (2018), pp. 401–416.

## Chapter 3

[1]  Thomas Britton, 'Not just acceptable, but beneficial: A modern case for the monarchy', *The Oxford Blue*, 4 June 2023, https://theoxfordblue.co.uk/not-just-acceptable-but-beneficial-a-modern-case-for-the-monarchy/.

[2]  BMG Research, 'NHS at 75: The NHS beats the royal family as top British symbol', 5 July 2023, https://www.bmgresearch.co.uk/the-nhs-beats-the-royal-family-as-top-british-symbol/#:~:text=The%20symbol%20that%20the%20public,Jack%20and%20even%20the%20pub.

[3]  Connor Ibbetson, 'What is the best thing about Britain, according to Britons?', YouGov, 30 May 2022, https://yougov.co.uk/society/articles/42672-what-best-thing-about-britain-according-britons?redirect_from=%2Ftopics%2Fsociety%2Farticles-reports%2F2022%2F05%2F30%2Fwhat-best-thing-about-britain-according-britons.

[4]  Matthew Smith, 'Where does public opinion stand on the monarchy ahead of the coronation?', YouGov, 3 May 2023, https://yougov.co.uk/society/articles/45654-where-does-public-opinion-stand-monarchy-ahead-cor?redirect_from=%2Ftopics%2Fsociety%2Farticles-reports%2F2023%2F05%2F03%2Fwhere-does-public-opinion-stand-monarchy-ahead-cor.

[5]  Jim MacLaughlin, *Re-imagining the Nation State* (Pluto Press, 2001), p. 2.

[6]  Benedict Anderson, *Imagined Communities* (Verso, 2006 [1983]).

7   Michael Billig, *Talking of the Royal Family* (Routledge, 1992),
    p. 34.
8   Andrzej Olechnowicz, *The Monarchy and the British Nation*
    (Cambridge University Press, 2007), p. 34.
9   Eloise Feilden, 'Top 10 most popular pub names in the UK', *The
    Drinks Business*, 1 June 2022, https://www.thedrinksbusiness.
    com/2022/06/top-10-most-popular-pub-names-in-the-uk/.
10  Tim Edensor, *National Identity, Popular Culture and Everyday Life*
    (Berg, 2002), p. 188.
11  Amanda Hyde, 'What the royal family is really worth to Britain',
    *Daily Telegraph*, 17 May 2023, https://www.telegraph.co.uk/travel/
    destinations/europe/united-kingdom/what-the-royal-family-is-
    really-worth-to-britain/.
12  Republic, 'Tourism', https://www.republic.org.uk/tourism.
13  'Visitors to Versailles', https://en.chateauversailles.fr/news/
    patronage-news/visitors-versailles-1682-1789#versailles-a-royal-
    destination.
14  This is also, as we know, not true. Although brief, we have had a
    republican nation before.
15  Isabelle Kirk, 'Platinum Jubilee: Where does public opinion stand
    on the monarchy?', YouGov, 1 June 2022, https://yougov.co.uk/
    society/articles/42695-platinum-jubilee-where-does-public-opinion-
    stand-m.
16  Sophie K. Rosa, 'Generation precariat: What's it like to feel robbed
    of your future?', *Novara*, 21 April 2022, https://novaramedia.
    com/2022/04/21/generation-precariat-whats-it-like-to-feel-robbed-
    of-your-future/.
17  Laura Clancy, *Running the Family Firm* (Manchester University
    Press, 2021).
18  Matthew Smith, 'Kate Middleton now the UK's most popular
    royal', YouGov, 9 April 2024, https://yougov.co.uk/politics/
    articles/49089-kate-middleton-now-uks-most-popular-royal.
19  *France 24*, 'Harry and Meghan go straight to work after lavish
    wedding', 20 May 2018, https://www.france24.com/en/20180520-
    harry-meghan-go-straight-work-after-lavish-wedding-0.
20  Afua Hirsch, 'Why a royal Meghan Markle matters', *TIME*,
    17 May 2018, https://time.com/5281096/meghan-markle-
    multicultural-britain/.
21  Clancy, *Running the Family Firm.*
22  Michael Savage, 'Scottish support for monarchy falls to 45 per
    cent, poll reveals', *The Guardian*, 15 May 2022, https://www.

theguardian.com/uk-news/2022/may/15/scottish-support-for-monarchy-falls-to-45-poll-reveals.

23 Tanya Abraham, 'What do ethnic minority Britons think of the monarchy and royal family?', YouGov, 3 May 2023, https://yougov.co.uk/society/articles/45655-what-do-ethnic-minority-britons-think-monarchy-and?redirect_from=%2Ftopics%2Fsociety%2Farticles-reports%2F2023%2F05%2F03%2Fwhat-do-ethnic-minority-britons-think-monarchy-and.

24 Catherine Craven and Elena Zambelli, 'Subject to change', *The Sociological Review*, 4 April 2023, https://thesociologicalreview.org/magazine/april-2023/post-elizabethan-futures/subject-to-change/.

25 Edensor, *National Identity*, p. 188.

26 Sherrylyn Clarke, 'Countdown to a republic: Royal place names', *Nation News*, 29 November 2021, https://nationnews.com/2021/11/29/countdown-republic-royal-place-names/.

27 David Mitchell, 'From Queen Elizabeth to King Charles: How Northern Ireland's unionists feel about the monarchy', *The Conversation*, 21 September 2022, https://theconversation.com/from-queen-elizabeth-to-king-charles-how-northern-irelands-unionists-feel-about-the-monarchy-190997.

28 Kirsty O'Rourke, 'The origins of Sinn Féin', *The History of Parliament*, 12 September 2023, https://thehistoryofparliament.wordpress.com/2023/09/12/the-origins-of-sinn-fein/.

29 'Royal family favourability', YouGov, 20 June 2023, https://docs.cdn.yougov.com/352czzbxah/Internal_RoyalFavourability_230608.pdf.

30 Savage, 'Scottish support for monarchy falls to 45 per cent, poll reveals'.

31 Linda Colley, *Britons* (Pimlico, 1992).

32 David Marquand, quoted in David McCrone, 'Scotland and the union', in David Morley and Kevin Robins, *British Cultural Studies* (Oxford University Press, 2001), p. 99.

33 *STV News*, 'When a post box was blown up in row over Queen's Scottish title', 28 November 2022, https://news.stv.tv/east-central/pillar-box-war-when-an-edinburgh-post-box-was-bombed-in-row-over-queen-elizabeth-ii-eiir-insignia.

34 Xander Elliards, 'Majority of Scots think monarchy is "mostly an English thing"', *The National*, 3 May 2023, https://www.thenational.scot/news/23497399.majority-scots-think-monarchy-mostly-english-thing/.

35  John Curtice, 'Another look at attitudes to the monarchy', *What Scotland Thinks*, 4 May 2023, https://www.whatscotlandthinks. org/2023/05/another-look-at-attitudes-to-the-monarchy/.

36  Joanna Morris, 'Do Scots want to keep the monarchy in an independent Scotland?', YouGov, 11 October 2022, https://yougov. co.uk/politics/articles/44013-do-scots-want-keep-monarchy-independent-scotland?redirect_from=%2Ftopics%2Fpolitics%2F articles-reports%2F2022%2F10%2F11%2Fdo-scots-want-keep-monarchy-independent-scotland.

37  Matthew Smith, 'Who are the monarchists', YouGov, 18 May 2018, https://yougov.co.uk/politics/articles/20809-who-are-monarchists.

38  Sam Whitworth, 'Corbyn jeered as he attacks royal family in insult to Queen "needs a bit of improvement"', *Daily Express*, 20 November 2019, https://www.express.co.uk/news/uk/1206665/ election-2019-news-jeremy-corbyn-labour-boris-johnson-itv-leadership-debate-queen.

39  John Ellis, 'The prince and the dragon: Welsh national identity and the 1911 investiture of the Prince of Wales', *Welsh History Review*, 18(2) (1996), pp. 272–295.

40  Eric Hobsbawm and Terence Ranger (eds), *The Invention of Tradition* (Cambridge University Press, 1983).

41  David Deans, 'Prince of Wales has no plans for investiture', BBC, 16 November 2022, https://www.bbc.co.uk/news/uk-wales-politics-63635177.

## Chapter 4

1  Simon Jenkins, 'Our monarchy is powerless and would remain that way under King Charles', *The Guardian*, 5 February 2015, https://www.theguardian.com/commentisfree/2015/feb/05/ monarchy-powerless-king-charles-opinions.

2  Rosalind Coward, *Female Desires* (Random House, 1985).

3  Tom Nairn, *The Enchanted Glass* (Verso, 2011 [1994]), p. 35.

4  Andre Rhoden-Paul and Sean Coughlan, 'Catherine, Princess of Wales, in hospital after abdominal surgery', BBC News, 17 January 2024, https://www.bbc.co.uk/news/uk-68009259.

5  David Bauder, 'The British royal family learns that if you don't fill an information vacuum, someone else will', *AP News*, 27 March 2024, https://apnews.com/article/princess-kate-cancer-media-online-internet-49d725512152e60d8fbe7bd093b8d5c6.

6   Naledi Ushe, 'AFP says Kensington Palace is no longer trusted source', *USA Today*, 15 March 2024, https://eu.usatoday.com/story/entertainment/celebrities/2024/03/15/princess-kate-photo-editing-scandal-afp-kill-notice-rift/72983672007/.

7   @KensingtonRoyal, 'Like many amateur photographers …', Twitter, 11 March 2024, https://twitter.com/KensingtonRoyal/status/1767135566645092616.

8   Mehera Bonner, 'The person who filmed Kate Middleton's farm shop video speaks out', *Cosmopolitan*, 19 March 2024, https://www.cosmopolitan.com/entertainment/celebs/a60241271/kate-middleton-farm-shop-video-real-or-fake/.

9   Sean Coughlan, 'Kate, Princess of Wales: I am having cancer treatment', BBC News, 23 March 2024, https://www.bbc.co.uk/news/uk-68641441.

10  Lauren Sarner, 'Prince William's alleged affair with Rose Hanbury gets late-night treatment', *NY Post*, 13 March 2024, https://nypost.com/2024/03/13/entertainment/prince-williams-alleged-affair-with-rose-hanbury-gets-late-night-treatment-amid-kate-drama/.

11  Frank Prochaska, *The Eagle and the Crown: Americans and the British Monarchy* (Yale University Press, 2008).

12  Lydia Brauer and Vickie Rutledge Shields, 'Princess Diana's celebrity in freezeframe', *European Journal of Cultural Studies*, 2 (1999), pp. 5–25.

13  Laura Clancy, '"If you do hold them to account, are you going to find yourself hitting more brick walls later?": Royal correspondents and royal news production', *Journalism*, 25(6), (2023), pp. 1328–1345.

14  Paul Moorhouse and David Cannadine, *The Queen: Art and Image* (National Portrait Gallery Publications, 2012).

15  Michael Streeter, 'The queen bows to her subjects', *The Independent*, 5 September 1997, http://www.independent.co.uk/news/the-queen-bows-to-her-subjects-1237450.html.

16  Afua Hagan, '25 years after Diana's death, has the public accepted Camilla?', *CTV News*, 30 August 2022, https://www.ctvnews.ca/world/25-years-after-diana-s-death-has-the-public-accepted-camilla-1.6046629.

17  *Reinventing the Royals*, BBC, dir. Steve Hewlett, 19 February 2015.

18  Kiko Itasaka, 'Camilla at 70: Has the duchess finally won British hearts?', NBC, 16 July 2017, https://www.nbcnews.com/news/world/camilla-70-has-duchess-finally-won-british-hearts-n783301.

19  Chris Rojek, *Celebrity* (Reaktion Books, 2001), pp. 13–14.

[20] Nick Couldry, 'Everyday royal celebrity', in David Morley and Kevin Robins (eds) *British Cultural Studies: Geography, Nationality, Identity* (Oxford University Press, 2001), pp. 221–234.

[21] Laura Clancy, '"Queen's day – TV's day": The British monarchy and the media industries', *Contemporary British History*, 33(3) (2019), pp. 427–450.

[22] Raymond Williams, *Keywords* (Fontana, 1976).

[23] Ibid.

[24] Ben Pimlott, *The Queen*, 2nd edn (Harper Press, 2012), p. 526.

[25] Daniel Roseman, 'Was this the day when royalty lost the plot?', *The Independent*, 21 April 1996, http://www.independent.co.uk/news/uk/home-news/was-this-the-day-whenroyalty-lost-the-plot-1305932.html.

[26] Chris Greer and Eugene McLaughlin, 'Why becoming a national treasure matters: Elite celebrity status and inequality in the United Kingdom', *European Journal of Cultural Studies*, 23(1) (2020), pp. 71–88.

## Chapter 5

[1] Robert Jobson, 'Prince William reveals why the royal family do charity work', *Evening Standard*, 23 January 2018, https://www.standard.co.uk/news/uk/prince-william-reveals-why-the-royal-family-do-charity-work-a3747496.html.

[2] Frank Prochaska, *Royal Bounty* (Yale University Press, 1995).

[3] Royal.uk, 'Charities and patronages', https://www.royal.uk/charities-and-patronages-1.

[4] Royal.uk, 'Garden parties', https://www.royal.uk/garden-parties.

[5] Prochaska, *Royal Bounty*.

[6] Ibid, p. 8.

[7] Ibid.

[8] Laura Clancy, *Running the Family Firm: How the Monarchy Manages its Image and Our Money* (Manchester University Press, 2021).

[9] Royal.uk, 'A speech by the Queen on her 21st birthday, 1947', https://www.royal.uk/21st-birthday-speech-21-april-1947.

[10] Alex Thomas, 'What the Queen's reign teaches the civil service', Institute for Government, 15 September 2022, https://www.instituteforgovernment.org.uk/article/comment/what-queens-reign-teaches-civil-service.

[11] Rob Whiteman, 'Queen Elizabeth II was devoted to being a public servant until the end', *Forbes*, 15 September 2022, https://www.

forbes.com/sites/robwhiteman/2022/09/15/queen-elizabeth-ii-was-devoted-to-being-a-public-servant-until-the-end/.

12   Kerra Maddern, 'Queen Elizabeth II seen as British "hero" – study shows', *Exeter News*, 4 May 2023, https://news.exeter.ac.uk/faculty-of-humanities-arts-and-social-sciences/queen-elizabeth-ii-seen-as-british-hero-study-shows/.

13   Tobias Harper, *From Servants of the Empire to Everyday Heroes* (Oxford University Press, 2020).

14   Prochaska, *Royal Bounty*.

15   Stephen Delahunty, 'Royal patronages provide no discernible benefits to charities', Third Sector, 16 July 2020, https://www.thirdsector.co.uk/royal-patronages-provide-no-discernible-benefits-charities-research-concludes/communications/article/1689654.

16   Linsey McGoey, *No Such Thing as a Free Gift* (Verso, 2015).

17   Jessica Sklair and Luna Glucksberg, 'Philanthrocapitalism as wealth management strategy: Philanthropy, inheritance and succession planning among the global elite', *The Sociological Review*, 69(2) (2021), pp. 314–329.

18   Pierre Bourdieu, *The Logic of Practice* (Stanford University Press, 1990).

19   Jo Littler, 'The new Victorians? Celebrity charity and the demise of the welfare state', *Celebrity Studies*, 6(4) (2015), p. 482.

20   Royal.uk, 'The Big Help Out', 8 May 2023, https://www.royal.uk/news-and-activity/2023-05-08/the-big-help-out.

21   Amelia Hill, 'Volunteering in sharp decline in England since Covid pandemic', *The Guardian*, 2 May 2023, https://www.theguardian.com/society/2023/may/02/volunteering-in-sharp-decline-in-england-since-covid-pandemic.

22   Laura Elston, 'Multimillion-pound coronation "a slap in the face"', *The Independent*, 9 May 2023, https://www.independent.co.uk/life-style/royal-family/how-much-coronation-cost-2023-b2335324.html.

23   Anoosh Chakelian, 'Replacing lost Sure Start centres is a tacit admission of austerity's failure', *New Statesman*, 10 February 2023, https://www.newstatesman.com/thestaggers/2023/02/replacing-lost-sure-start-centres-is-a-tacit-admission-of-austeritys-failure.

24   Hill, 'Volunteering in sharp decline'.

25   Emma Dowling, *The Care Crisis* (Verso, 2021).

26   Royal College of Nursing, 'Valuing nursing in the UK', 13 February 2023, https://www.rcn.org.uk/Professional-Development/publications/valuing-nursing-in-the-uk-uk-pub-010-695.

27 Saskia Rowlands, 'NHS workers get special King's Coronation invite', *Mirror*, 15 April 2023, https://www.mirror.co.uk/news/royals/nhs-workers-special-kings-coronation-29721717.

28 Raka Shome, *Diana and Beyond: White Femininity, National Identity, and Contemporary Media Culture* (University of Illinois Press, 2014), p. 118.

29 Ibid.

## Chapter 6

1 Ben Domenech, 'The ignorance of Queen Elizabeth's "anti-colonialist" critics', *History Reclaimed*, 22 September 2022, https://historyreclaimed.co.uk/the-ignorance-of-queen-elizabeths-anti-colonialist-critics/.

2 Laura Clancy, '"If you move in the same circles as the royals, then you'll get stories about them": Royal correspondents, cultural intermediaries and class', *Cultural Sociology*, 17(3) (2023), pp. 331–350.

3 Tony Batchelor, '"Tone deaf": Optics of William and Kate's Jamaica tour questioned after photos draw ridicule', *The Independent*, 23 March 2022, https://www.independent.co.uk/news/uk/home-news/william-kate-jamaica-royals-b2042682.html.

4 Rachel Hall and Amelia Gentleman, '"Perfect storm": Royals misjudged Caribbean tour, say critics', *The Guardian*, 25 March 2022, https://www.theguardian.com/uk-news/2022/mar/25/william-and-kate-caribbean-tour-slavery-reparations-royals.

5 Basil Morgan, 'Sir John Hawkins', *Oxford Dictionary of National Biography*, 4 October 2007, https://www.oxforddnb.com/display/10.1093/ref:odnb/9780198614128.001.0001/odnb-9780198614128-e-12672.

6 Nick Robins, *The Corporation That Changed the World* (Pluto Press, 2012).

7 Karla Adams, 'A crown branded onto bodies links British monarchy to slave trade', *NAARC*, 29 September 2023, https://reparationscomm.org/reparations-news/slave-trade-monarchy-uk-archives/.

8 Ibid.

9 William A. Pettigrew, *Freedom's Debt* (University of North Carolina Press, 2013).

10 Richard Dunn, *Sugar and Slaves* (University of North Carolina Press, 1972), p. 160.

11  Brooke Newman, *The Queen's Silence* (Mariner, forthcoming 2025).

12  Miles Taylor, *Empress: Queen Victoria and India* (Yale University Press, 2018).

13  Museum of British Colonialism, 'Crowning the coloniser', 22 April 2023, https://museumofbritishcolonialism.org/2023-4-22-monarchy-and-empire-victoria/.

14  Robert Aldrich and Cindy McCreery, *Royals on Tour* (Manchester University Press, 2018).

15  William Dalrymple and Anita Anand, *Koh-i-Noor: The History of the World's Most Infamous Diamond* (Bloomsbury Publishing, 2017).

16  Press Association, 'Lucy Worsley launches review into royal palaces' links to slave trade', *The Independent*, 28 October 2020, https://www.independent.co.uk/news/uk/home-news/lucy-worsley-historic-royal-palaces-review-slave-trade-kensington-palace-tower-of-london-hampton-court-b1391904.html.

17  Adams, 'A crown branded onto bodies'.

18  Corinne Fowler, *Green Unpleasant Lands* (Peepal Tree Press, 2020).

19  Laura Clancy and Sara de Benedictis, '"I wanted to offer my sympathy … woman to woman": Reading The Crown during a conjuncture of crisis', *Soundings*, 79 (2021), pp. 122–133.

20  Commonwealth, 'About us', https://thecommonwealth.org/about-us.

21  Laura Clancy, 'Who told Prince Charles he could be head of the Commonwealth?', *The Conversation*, 25 November 2015, https://theconversation.com/who-told-prince-charles-he-could-be-head-of-the-commonwealth-51271.

22  Archie Bland, 'Monday briefing: The Commonwealth countries considering a republican future', *The Guardian*, 12 September 2022, https://www.theguardian.com/world/2022/sep/12/monday-briefing-commonwealth-charles-first-edition.

23  Holly Randell-Moon, 'Thieves like us: The British monarchy, celebrity, and settler colonialism', *Celebrity Studies*, 8(3) (2017), pp. 393–408.

24  Ibid.

25  Danya Hajjaji, 'Prince William carried on throne photo resurfaces', *Newsweek*, 12 March 2021, https://www.newsweek.com/prince-william-carried-throne-photo-resurfaces-after-royal-says-family-not-racist-1575701.

26    Chris Jancelewicz, 'Prince Charles and Camilla laugh during Inuit throat-singing performance', *Global News*, 4 July 2017, https://globalnews.ca/news/3573437/prince-charles-camilla-inuit-throat-singing-iqaluit/#:~:text=Charles%2C%2068%2C%20and%20Camilla%2C,re%20laughing%20about%20the%20performance.

27    Edward Said, *Orientalism* (Pantheon, 1978).

28    Le Monde, 'Jamaica and Belize consider becoming republics ahead of King Charles' coronation', *Le Monde*, 4 May 2023, https://www.lemonde.fr/en/international/article/2023/05/04/jamaica-and-belize-consider-becoming-republics-ahead-of-king-charles-coronation_6025461_4.html.

29    Chris Leadbeater, 'How Queen Victoria left her mark on every corner of the planet', *Daily Telegraph*, 24 May 2019, https://www.telegraph.co.uk/travel/lists/places-named-after-queen-victoria/.

30    Emily Wind, 'Captain Cook statue sawn off and Queen Victoria monument defaced in Melbourne on eve of 26 January', *The Guardian*, 24 January 2024, https://www.theguardian.com/australia-news/2024/jan/25/captain-cook-statue-toppled-in-st-kilda-on-eve-of-26-jaunary.

31    Frantz Fanon, *The Wretched of the Earth* (Grove Press, 1963), p. 50.

32    Cabinet Office, 'Global Britain in a competitive age', Policy Paper, 2 July 2021, https://www.gov.uk/government/publications/global-britain-in-a-competitive-age-the-integrated-review-of-security-defence-development-and-foreign-policy/global-britain-in-a-competitive-age-the-integrated-review-of-security-defence-development-and-foreign-policy.

33    Gurminder K Bhambra and John Holmwood, 'Colonialism, postcolonialism and the liberal welfare state', *New Political Economy*, 23(5) (2018), pp. 574–587.

34    Imogen Tyler, *Stigma* (Zed, 2020).

35    Stefanie Lehner, 'Subaltern Scotland: Devolution and postcoloniality', in Berthold Schoene (ed), *Edinburgh Companion to Contemporary Scottish Literature* (Edinburgh University Press, 2007), pp. 292–300.

36    Gurminder K. Bhambra, 'Relations of extraction, relations of redistribution: Empire, nation, and the construction of the British welfare state', *The British Journal of Sociology*, 73, (2022), pp. 4–15 (emphasis in original), and the following quote.

## Chapter 7

1   Ross Clark, 'Fretting over "land inequality" is a waste of time', *The Spectator*, 18 April 2019, https://www.spectator.co.uk/article/fretting-over-land-inequality-is-a-waste-of-time/.

2   Guy Shrubsole, *Who Owns England?* (William Collins, 2019).

3   Ibid.

4   Brett Christophers, *Rentier Capitalism* (Verso, 2020).

5   Rob Evans, 'Half of England is owned by less than 1% of the population', *The Guardian*, 17 April 2019, https://www.theguardian.com/money/2019/apr/17/who-owns-england-thousand-secret-landowners-author.

6   Gregory Clark and Neil Cummins. 'Intergenerational wealth mobility in England, 1858–2012', *Economic Journal*, 125 (2015), pp. 61–85.

7   Cahal Milmo, 'Billionaire Duke of Westminster leaves vast fortune to 25-year-old-son', *iNews*, 10 August 2016, https://inews.co.uk/news/i-wanted-joe-bloggs-billionaire-duke-westminster-leaves-vast-fortune-25-year-old-son-17592.

8   The Crown Estate, 'The Crown Estate announces record £442.6 million net revenue', 29 June 2023, https://www.thecrownestate.co.uk/news/the-crown-estate-announces-record-gbp442-6-million-net-revenue-profit-for.

9   The Crown Estate, *Integrated Annual Report and Accounts 2022/2023*, https://downloads.ctfassets.net/nv65su7t80y5/62CIdZeDjs0I178w13bZh1/378d9e004247ff8a2fcf19e881a6f0e3/tce_ar23_web_accessible.pdf.

10  Ibid.

11  The Crown Estate, 'About us', https://www.thecrownestate.co.uk/about-us.

12  John Lubbock, 'Defund the Queen', *Tribune*, 26 March 2021, https://tribunemag.co.uk/2021/03/defund-the-queen.

13  Shrubsole, *Who Owns England?*

14  Rob Evans and David Pegg, '£187m of Windsor family wealth hidden in secret royal wills', *The Guardian*, 18 July 2022, https://www.theguardian.com/uk-news/2022/jul/18/187m-pounds-of-windsor-family-wealth-hidden-in-secret-royal-wills.

15  Wild Card, 'How much land do the royals own?', https://www.wildcard.land/how-much-land-do-the-royals-own.html#:~:text=Land%20privately%20owned%20by%20the,Delnadamph%20Estate%2C%207000%20acres).

16  What Do they Know, 'How many acres of land', 8 December 2017, https://www.whatdotheyknow.com/request/how_many_acres_of_land.

17  Who Owns England, 'What land does the Duchy of Cornwall own?', 15 March 2017, https://whoownsengland.org/2017/03/15/what-land-does-the-duchy-of-cornwall-own/.

18  Neil Tague, 'Here's what the new King owns in the North West', *Place North West*, 9 September 2022, https://www.placenorthwest.co.uk/heres-what-the-new-king-owns-in-the-north-west/.

19  Graham Smith, 'What's behind King Charles's bumper pay rise?', *The Guardian*, 22 July 2023, https://www.theguardian.com/commentisfree/2023/jul/22/royal-secrecy-public-money-crown-estate-king-charles.

20  Laura Clancy, *Running the Family Firm: How the Monarchy Manages its Image and Our Money* (Manchester University Press, 2021).

21  Ibid.

22  Felicity Lawrence and Rob Evans, 'Who owns and profits from the duchies of Lancaster and Cornwall?', *The Guardian*, 5 April 2023, https://www.theguardian.com/uk-news/2023/apr/05/who-owns-and-profits-from-the-duchies-of-lancaster-and-cornwall-timeline?CMP=share_btn_url, and the following quote.

23  House of Commons Committee of Public Accounts, 'The accounts of the Duchies of Cornwall and Lancaster', nineteenth report of the session 2004–5, 21 July 2005, https://publications.parliament.uk/pa/cm200405/cmselect/cmpubacc/313/313.pdf.

24  Rob Evans, Felicity Lawrence and David Pegg, 'Revealed: Royals took more than £1bn income from controversial estates', *The Guardian*, 5 April 2023, https://www.theguardian.com/uk-news/ng-interactive/2023/apr/05/revealed-royals-took-more-than-1bn-income-from-controversial-estates-king-charles-queen-duchies-cornwall-lancaster.

25  Brett Christophers, 'The rentierization of the United Kingdom economy', *Environment and Planning A: Economy and Space*, 55(6) (2023), pp. 1438–1470.

26  Lisa Adkins, Melinda Cooper and Martijn Konings, *The Asset Economy* (Polity, 2020).

27  Shrubsole, *Who Owns England?*

28  Evans et al, 'Revealed'.

29  Jake, 'The Earl & Countess of Devon', *One Magazine*, 21 May 2018, https://www.one-mag.co.uk/the-earl-countess-of-devon/

30  BBC News, 'Duchy of Cornwall criticised over Isle of Scilly property management', 23 March 2020, https://www.bbc.co.uk/news/uk-england-cornwall-51960855.

31  Rob Evans, David Pegg and Michael Barton, 'Prince Charles vetted laws that stop his tenants buying their homes', *The Guardian*, 9 February 2021, https://www.theguardian.com/uk-news/2021/feb/09/prince-charles-vetted-laws-that-stop-his-tenants-buying-their-homes.

32  Robert Booth, 'Duchy of Cornwall residents fight "unfair" freehold ban', *The Guardian*, 11 September 2017, https://www.theguardian.com/uk-news/2017/sep/11/duchy-of-cornwall-residents-fight-freehold-ban-prince-charles.

33  Chris Bryant, *Entitled* (Doubleday, 2017).

34  Mike Savage, *Social Class in the 21st Century* (Penguin, 2015).

35  Clancy, *Running the Family Firm*.

36  Aaron Reeves, Sam Friedman, Charles Rahal and Magne Flemmen, 'The decline and persistence of the old boy: Private schools and elite recruitment 1897 to 2016', *American Sociological Review*, 82(6) (2017) pp. 1139–1166.

37  Pierre Bourdieu, *Distinction* (Harvard University Press, 1984).

## Chapter 8

1  *Radio Times*, 'Portraying the Queen on screen', 3 June 2022, https://www.radiotimes.com/tv/queen-actors-radio-times-magazine/.

2  David Loades, *Elizabeth I: The Golden Reign of Gloriana* (The National Archives, 2003).

3  Christopher Haigh, *Elizabeth I*, 2nd edn (Longman Pearson, 2000), p. 24.

4  Louis Montrose, *The Subject of Elizabeth* (University of Chicago Press, 2006), p. 149.

5  Diane Roberts, 'The body of the princess', in Alfred J. Lopez (ed), *Postcolonial Whiteness* (State University of New York Press, 2005).

6  Roberts, 'The body of the princess', p. 32.

7  Margaret Homans, *Royal Representations* (University of Chicago Press, 1998).

8  Raka Shome, *Diana and Beyond* (University of Illinois Press, 2014), p. 40.

9  Jemima Repo and Riina Yrjölä, 'The gender politics of celebrity humanitarianism in Africa', *International Feminist Journal of Politics*, 13(1) (2011), pp. 44–62.

10    Peggy McIntosh, 'White privilege: Unpacking the invisible knapsack', *Peace and Freedom Magazine*, July/August 1989, pp. 10–12.

11    Laura Clancy and Hannah Yelin, '"Meghan's manifesto": Meghan Markle and the co-option of feminism', *Celebrity Studies*, 11(3) (2018), pp. 372–377.

12    BBC News, 'Danny Baker fired by BBC over royal baby chimp tweet', 9 May 2019, https://www.bbc.co.uk/news/entertainment-arts-48212693.

13    Kehinde Andrews, 'The post-racial princess: Delusions of racial progress and intersectional failures', *Women's Studies International Forum*, 84 (2021), p. 2.

14    Hilary Mantel, 'Royal bodies', *London Review of Books*, 35(4) (February 2013), https://www.lrb.co.uk/the-paper/v35/n04/hilary-mantel/royal-bodies.

15    Rachel J. Weil, *'The Politics of Legitimacy: Women and the Warming-Pan Scandal': The Revolution of 1688–1689: Changing Perspectives*, ed. Lois G. Schwoerer (Cambridge University Press, 1992).

16    Esther Adley, 'Pregnant Kate: After months of gossip and false claims, this time it's official', *The Guardian*, 3 December 2012, https://www.theguardian.com/uk/2012/dec/03/pregnant-kate-gossip-false-claims.

17    Shome, *Diana and Beyond*, p. 23.

18    Historic Royal Palaces, 'LGBT+ royal histories', https://www.hrp.org.uk/tower-of-london/history-and-stories/lgbt-royal-histories/#gs.bdm6c4.

19    *Grazia*, 'The courage of a king', https://graziamagazine.com/us/articles/lord-ivars-journey-to-marrying-james-coyle/.

20    Laura Clancy and Hannah Yelin, 'Monarchy is a feminist issue: Andrew, Meghan and #MeToo era monarchy', *Women's Studies International Forum*, 84 (2021), pp. 1–8.

21    Antony Clements-Thrower, 'MP's wife had affair with playboy prince then was locked in asylum for rest of her life', *Mirror*, 6 June 2023, https://www.mirror.co.uk/news/weird-news/mps-wife-affair-playboy-prince-30165342.

22    'Prince Andrew & the Epstein scandal', *Newsnight*, 16 November 2019.

23    Robert Booth, 'Jimmy Savile caused concern with behaviour on visits to Prince Charles', *The Guardian*, 29 October 2012, https://www.theguardian.com/media/2012/oct/29/jimmy-savile-

behaviour-prince-charles; Martin Robinson, 'Jimmy Savile's media handbook for the royals: Secret letters reveal how paedophile DJ advised Prince Charles to set up "incident room" with teletext after heir begged him for help to boost family's PR image after Andrew Lockerbie gaffe', *Daily Mail*, 6 April 2022, https://www.dailymail.co.uk/news/article-10691091/Pictured-begging-letters-exchanged-Prince-Charles-Jimmy-Savile.html.

24    Holly Bancroft, 'Queen "to spend millions funding Prince Andrew's defence against sex abuse claims"', *The Independent*, 2 October 2021, https://www.independent.co.uk/news/uk/home-news/queen-prince-andrew-epstein-millions-legal-case-b1931084.html.

25    Victoria Ward and Josie Ensor, 'Queen to help pay for £12m Prince Andrew settlement', *Daily Telegraph*, 15 February 2022, https://www.telegraph.co.uk/royal-family/2022/02/15/queen-help-pay-12m-prince-andrew-settlement/.

26    Clancy and Yelin, 'Monarchy is a feminist issue'.

## Conclusion

1    Republic, 'Arrested coronation protesters: One year on', https://www.republic.org.uk/arrested_coronation_protesters_one_year_on.

2    Niamh Kennedy, 'Anti-monarchy protesters arrested ahead of King Charles' coronation', *CNN*, 6 May 2023, https://edition.cnn.com/2023/05/06/uk/king-charles-anti-monarchy-protest-arrests-ckc-gbr-intl/index.html.

3    Lucia Binding, 'Royal fan detained for 13 hours after "wrongful arrest" at king's coronation', *Sky*, 12 May 2023, https://news.sky.com/story/royal-fan-detained-for-13-hours-after-wrongful-arrest-at-kings-coronation-12878740#:~:text=Alice%20Chambers%20was%20an%20innocent,up%20for%20the%20whole%20day.

4    Amnesty International, 'UK: Government plan to push more anti-protest legislation through Lords must be stopped', 7 June 2023, https://www.amnesty.org.uk/press-releases/uk-government-plan-push-more-anti-protest-legislation-through-lords-must-be-stopped#:~:text=In%20April%20this%20year%2C%20the,Crime%2C%20Sentencing%20and%20Courts%20Act.

5    Rivkah Brown, 'If we can't change the law, we'll break it', Novara, 16 March 2021, https://novaramedia.com/2021/03/16/our-right-to-protest-is-under-threat-but-we-can-fightback/.

6    Barney Davis, 'Man with blank sheet of paper threatened with arrest if he wrote "not my King" on it', *Evening Standard*,

12 September 2022, https://www.standard.co.uk/news/uk/police-arrest-blank-paper-king-charles-monarchy-b1025152.html.

7   Roy Greenslade, 'Jeremy Corbyn and the national anthem – a press chorus of disapproval', *The Guardian*, 16 September 2015, https://www.theguardian.com/media/greenslade/2015/sep/16/jeremy-corbyn-and-the-national-anthem-a-press-chorus-of-disapproval.

8   Josh Butler, 'Australian senator calls the Queen a coloniser while being sworn in to parliament', *The Guardian*, 1 August 2022, https://www.theguardian.com/australia-news/2022/aug/01/australian-greens-senator-lidia-thorpe-calls-queen-coloniser-while-being-sworn-into-parliament.

9   Michael Billig, *Banal Nationalism* (SAGE, 1995).

10  Christopher Silvester, 'For the monarchy's future, keep some royals at arm's length', *Politico*, 12 September 2022, https://www.politico.eu/article/uk-queen-elizabeth-king-charles-for-the-monarchys-future-keep-some-royals-at-arms-length/.

11  Liam James, 'King Charles "vows to have slimmed down coronation" amid cost of living crisis', *The Independent*, 21 September 2022, https://www.independent.co.uk/news/uk/home-news/king-charles-coronation-cost-crown-b2171646.html.

12  Matthew Davies, 'Who are Britain's working royals and where do they live?', *National News*, 30 April 2023, https://www.thenationalnews.com/world/uk-news/2023/04/30/who-are-britains-working-royals-and-where-do-they-live/.

13  John M.T. Balmer, Stephen A. Greyser and Mats Urde, 'The Crown as a corporate brand: Insights from monarchies', *Journal of Brand Management*, 14 (2006), pp. 137–161.

14  Andrew Anthony, 'The queen is dead, long live the king', *The Guardian*, 25 September 2022, https://www.theguardian.com/uk-news/2022/sep/25/queen-is-dead-long-live-king-british-monarchy-republicanism-charles.

15  Graham Smith, *Abolish the Monarchy* (Penguin Random House, 2023).

16  Republic, 'Parliamentary republics', https://www.republic.org.uk/parliamentary_republics.

17  Frank Prochaska, *The Republic of Britain* (Penguin, 2001).

18  Diane Purkiss, *The English Civil War* (Harper Perennial, 2007), and following.

19  Thomas Paine, *Rights of Man, Common Sense, and other Political Writings*, ed. Mark Philip (Oxford University Press, 1995), p. 230.

20  Prochaska, *The Republic of Britain*.

21 Karl Marx, *The Civil War in France* (London, 1933), p. 43.

22 Prochaska, *The Republic of Britain*, p. 186.

23 Martyn Rush, 'Tony Benn's plan to democratise Britain', *Tribune*, 26 February 2021, https://tribunemag.co.uk/2021/02/tony-benns-plan-to-democratise-britain-and-abolish-the-monarchy.

24 Sue Townsend, *The Queen and I* (Methuen, 1992).

25 Rush, 'Tony Benn'.

26 Allison O. Ramsay, 'The Barbados effect', *Sociological Review*, 4 April 2023, https://thesociologicalreview.org/magazine/april-2023/post-elizabethan-futures/the-barbados-effect/.

27 Daniel Sanderson, 'Scotland could ditch the monarchy', *Daily Telegraph*, 13 March 2023, https://www.telegraph.co.uk/news/2023/03/13/scotland-could-ditch-monarchy-within-five-years-leaving-uk-claims/.

# FURTHER READING

## Monarchy and anti-monarchism

Norman Baker, ... *And What Do You Do? What the Royal Family Don't Want You to Know* (Biteback, 2020).

Michael Billig, *Talking of the Royal Family* (Routledge, 1992).

Dennis Hardy, *Poundbury: The Town That Charles Built* (Town and Country Planning Association, 2006).

Homosexual Death Drive, *Poundbury: A Queer Tour of Monarchy* (33editions, 2023).

Human Resources, *Royally Flush*, 2-part podcast series (Broccoli Productions, January 2022).

Anna Keay, *The Restless Republic: Britain without a Crown* (William Collins, 2022).

David McClure, *The Queen's True Worth: Unravelling the Public & Private Finances of Elizabeth II* (Lume, 2020).

Philip Murphy, *The Empire's New Clothes: The Myth of the Commonwealth* (Hurst and Company, 2018).

Tom Nairn, *The Enchanted Glass: Britain and Its Monarchy*, updated edn (Vintage, 2011).

Brooke Newman, *The Queen's Silence* (Mariner, forthcoming 2025).

Cele C. Otnes and Pauline Maclaran, *Royal Fever: The British Monarchy in Consumer Culture* (University of California Press, 2015).

Edward Owens, *The Family Firm: Monarchy, Mass Media and the British Public, 1932–53* (Institute of Historical Research, 2019).

'Post-Elizabethan futures', *The Sociological Review Magazine Online* (April 2023).

Diane Purkiss, *The English Civil War: A People's History* (Harper Perennial, 2006).

Republic, *Royal Secrets: A Report on Royal Secrecy and Power*, report available on https://www.republic.org.uk/royal_secrets (2015).

Republic, 'The Man Who Shouldn't be King', available on YouTube, https://www.youtube.com/watch?v=TGamLrHlikc (27 March 2020).

Raka Shome, *Diana and Beyond: White Femininity, National Identity, and Contemporary Media Culture* (University of Illinois Press, 2014).

Graham Smith, *Abolish the Monarchy* (Penguin Random House, 2023).

Surviving Society, 'The Global Power of the British Monarchy', 6-part podcast series (Surviving Society Productions, 2023).

Puangchon Unchanam, *Royal Capitalism: Wealth, Class and Monarchy in Thailand* (The University of Wisconsin Press, 2020).

## The elites and the establishment

Chris Bryant, *Entitled: A Critical History of the British Aristocracy* (Transworld Publishers, 2017).

Aeron Davis, *Reckless Opportunists: Elites at the End of the Establishment* (Manchester University Press, 2018).

Jo Littler, *Against Meritocracy: Culture, Power and Myths of Mobility* (Routledge, 2017).

Andrew Sayer, *Why We Can't Afford the Rich* (Policy Press, 2015).

Guy Shrubsole, *Who Owns England? How We Lost Our Land and How to Take It Back* (William Collins, 2019).

## The British empire and (post-)colonialism

Kehinde Andrews, *The New Age of Empire: How Racism and Colonialism Still Rule the World* (Penguin, 2022).

Caroline Elkins, *Legacy of Violence: A History of the British Empire* (Vintage, 2023)

*Empire*, podcast hosted by William Dalrymple and Anita Anand (Goalhanger Podcasts, 2022–).

Paul Gilroy, *There Ain't No Black in the Union Jack* (Routledge, 1992).

Priyamvada Gopal, *Insurgent Empire: Anticolonial Resistance and British Dissent* (Verso, 2020).

David Olusoga, *Black and British: A Forgotten History* (Macmillan, 2016).

Shashi Tharoor, *Inglorious Empire: What the British Did to India* (Penguin, 2018).

# INDEX

References to figures are in *italics*;
references to tables and boxes are in **bold**.